Publishing in African Languages:
Challenges and Prospects

Bellagio Studies in Publishing

Philip G. Altbach, General Editor

Other titles in this series include:

1: Philip G. Altbach, editor, *Publishing in Africa and the Third World*

2: Carol Priestley, *Publishing Assistance Programs: Review and Inventory*

3: Philip G. Altbach and Hyaeweol Choi, *Bibliography on Publishing in the Third World, 1980–1993* (Published by Ablex Publishers, POB 811, Stamford, CT 06904, USA)

4: Philip G. Altbach, editor, *Copyright and Development: Inequality in the Information Age*

5: Urvashi Butalia and Ritu Menon, *Making a Difference: Feminist Publishing in the South*

6: Henry Chakava, *Publishing in Africa: One Man's Perspective*

7: Philip G. Altbach, editor, *The Challenge of the Market: Privatization and Publishing in Africa*

8: Philip G. Altbach and Damtew Teferra, editors, *Knowledge Dissemination in Africa: The Role of Scholarly Journals*

9: Philip G. Altbach and Damtew Teferra, editors, *Publishing and Development: A Book of Readings*

10: Philip G. Altbach and Damtew Teferra, editors, *Publishing in African Languages: Challenges and Prospects*

Publishing in African Languages:
Challenges and Prospects

Edited by
Philip G. Altbach and Damtew Teferra

Bellagio Studies in Publishing, 10

Bellagio Publishing Network
Research and Information Center
in association with Boston College
Center for International Higher Education
Chestnut Hill, Massachusetts USA

June 1999

© 1999 Bellagio Publishing Network

ISBN number: 0-9646078-5-9

Bellagio Studies in Publishing, 10

For further information about this publication, please contact:

Bellagio Publishing Network
Research and Information Center
207 Campion Hall
Boston College
Chestnut Hill, MA 02467, USA

Fax: (617) 552–8422

For information about the Bellagio Publishing Network, please contact:

Bellagio Publishing Network Secretariat
The Jam Factory
27 Park End Street
Oxford OX1 1HU, UK

Fax: 44–1865–244–584

Copies of this book may be purchased from:

African Books Collective, Ltd.
The Jam Factory
27 Park End Street
Oxford OX1 1HU, UK

Fax: 44–1865–793–298

Table of Contents

Preface Philip G. Altbach and Damtew Teferra	vii
1. The Dilemmas of Publishing in African Languages: A Comparative Perspective Philip G. Altbach	1
2. Publishing in Kiswahili: A Writer's Perspective M.M. Mulokozi	11
3. Publishing in Southern African Languages: History, Challenges, and Opportunities Dumisani K. Ntshangase	43
4. African Publishing and National Languages: The West African Experience Mamadou Aliou Sow	65
5. The Politics of Multilingual Education and Publishing in Ethiopia Damtew Teferra	75
6. Publishing in Local Languages in Nigeria: A Publisher's Perspective Victor U. Nwankwo	111
7. Publishing in Indian Languages: Perspectives from the Subcontinent Urvashi Butalia	129
8. World or Indigenous Languages? Influences on Language Policies for Publishing in Africa Thomas Clayton	145
Contributors	165

Preface

We are convinced that a significant part of the future of African publishing belongs to books written in African languages. It is this conviction that underlies this volume. Conversations with colleagues at the African Publishers Network (APNET) and others strengthened our view that African language publishing is a central issue. All of the authors in this book focus on the problems and the accomplishments of African language publishing. It is our aim to bring to readers a realistic appraisal of the current trends and future prospects concerning this topic. Doing this has not been an easy task. Not only are the issues complicated and multifaceted, but there is surprisingly little research available on African publishing. As with publishing in general, and publishing in developing countries particularly, there are few analysts concerned with understanding the underlying trends and issues pertinent to this field. We hope that *Publishing in African Languages* will contribute to our understanding and perhaps stimulate further thinking and analysis on this important topic.

A serious attempt has been made to reflect the state of indigenous language publishing across the entire African continent. Altbach provides an overall comparative analysis of the dilemmas of publishing in indigenous languages. He examines the issue of publishing in African languages by drawing from Asian, European, and Latin American countries that have embarked on this same journey. Mulokozi presents the indigenous publishing scenario from a writer's perspective. He bases his essay on writing in the Kiswahili language. Ntshangase discusses the history, challenges, and potential of publishing in southern African languages. He covers this part of Africa, which had four different colonial rulers, and examines their characteristic influence on indigenous languages. The general trend of indigenous publishing in French-speaking West Africa is presented by Sow. He discusses the challenges and potential of the Guinean experience with national languages and publishing. Teferra's article mainly dwells on Ethiopia's transition to multilingual education and the state of publishing necessary to make this possible. He also presents a broad account of the significance of moving to indigenous language education. Indigenous publishing experience from English-speaking West Africa comes from Nigeria—the most populous African country and one with several hundred languages. Nwankwo discusses this topic from a publisher's perspective.

African publishing does not exist in a vacuum. It is tied to international trends, and much can be learned from the experience of other countries. For these reasons, we have included an essay by Butalia on the Indian experience with indigenous language publishing. She portrays the rich history of indigenous language publishing in India—the world's second most-populous subcontinent and one with vast cultural and linguistic diversity—examining some of the subcontinent's major languages. Clayton places African language publishing in the context of the world knowledge system. He explores why the vast majority of books produced in and for use in Africa are written in world languages that are alien to the vast majority of the population.

We are indebted especially to the authors of the chapters in this book. Most are directly involved in publishing, and face the pressures of the book industry. David Engberg assisted us with editing and formatting. This book was sponsored by the Bellagio Publishing Network Research and Information Center, an organization funded by the Rockefeller Foundation. Additional support came from the Center for International Higher Education at Boston College.

Philip G. Altbach
Damtew Teferra
Chestnut Hill, Massachusetts
June 1999

1

The Dilemmas of Publishing in African Languages: A Comparative Perspective

Philip G. Altbach

Introduction

Few would argue with the value of making books available in indigenous languages. It would seem obvious that books should be available in languages spoken by large proportions of the population of a country or region. Yet, relatively little attention is paid to indigenous language publishing, and in many developing countries, in Africa and elsewhere, most books are published in foreign languages. The large majority of books published in Africa appear in English, French, Portuguese, or other non-African languages. I am concerned here with understanding some of the context of publishing books in indigenous languages, with a special focus on Africa. I will consider this topic in a comparative context since the experiences of other parts of the world are useful in understanding Africa.

Why Publish in Indigenous Languages?

Why even pose this question? It should be natural that books are published in the language or languages spoken in a country. Yet, the issue of the language of publication is one of lasting controversy. In many developing countries, most books are not published in the primary languages spoken by the majority of people. This is the case for virtually all of Sub-Saharan Africa. In India, despite active local language publishing, half the books are published in English. In the industrialized countries, the increasing use of English for scientific and scholarly communication is calling into question the use of such languages as Dutch, Norwegian, and Swedish as languages of science. Even in Germany, English is increasingly used for scholarly communication. In the countries of Central and Eastern Europe—where Russian was a key language during the Cold War period—debates are now under way as to the appropriate languages for research. For now, however, most books are published in the national language of the country.

In some industrialized nations, educators have debated the medium of instruction for higher education. In the Netherlands, Scandinavia, Hungary, and even Japan, English is used as a medium of instruction in some university courses. Debate about the appropriate language for publishing is widespread, and by no means limited to the developing countries. The question assumes special importance in developing countries because of their limited resources, the urgent needs of social and economic development, and the necessity of strengthening civil society.

The arguments for indigenous language publishing are convincing in the African context. If mass literacy is to be achieved, it must be in the languages that people speak—and read. Basic literacy materials must be available, as well as books, magazines, and other publications to ensure that literacy skills will be maintained. Women, who significantly benefit from literacy campaigns, need relevant reading materials in indigenous languages since in many countries they are less likely to have access to long-term schooling and hence to the metropolitan languages.

Communication is most effective when it is in the language of primary use. Local authorship is most likely in indigenous languages. The book market potential is greater in indigenous languages since the number of readers is larger than in foreign languages, although the purchasing power of potential buyers is generally low.

There has been much discussion of the role of civil society in developing countries. Civil society includes participation in governance and public affairs by the people, a trend toward democracy, growth of nongovernmental organizations, and the success of independent publishers, journals, and media. Participation in a civil society requires an informed population, and information requires both literacy and published material. Civil society requires publishers and a literate population able to buy the products of publishers and benefit from information and analysis. Publishing in indigenous languages is therefore an essential part of the growth of a civil society.

In any developing country, an independent publishing industry is necessarily anchored by the educational system. At the same time, the schools, as well as higher education institutions, depend on books and other published materials to fulfill their educational goals. A symbiotic but often unrecognized relationship exists between publishing and the educational system at all levels. Most agree that education in the mother tongue is most effective, especially at the primary levels, and there is a growing trend toward mother tongue education. In order for literacy in the mother tongue to be maintained and enhanced, reading materials in that language are required. This means that indigenous language publishing is central to the creation and maintenance of literacy and to the educational system.

The publishing industry is also dependent on the educational system. In developing countries, schools are by far the largest purchasers of books. Indeed, textbooks comprise the largest segment of the publishing market. Textbooks are increasingly being published in indigenous languages, which creates a potential link between the market for school books and a broader market for books in indigenous languages. Too often, there are insufficient connections between textbook publishers and publishers of books for the general market. Now that the private sector is increasingly taking over responsibility for textbook production from government agencies, the potential for such connections is enhanced. Not only has the public sector generally failed to produce books efficiently, it has robbed the publishing industry of the most lucrative part of publishing in developing countries. The trend toward the privatization of textbook production will strengthen indigenous publishing and provide it with a stronger economic base, although a conscious policy of linking textbook and general publishing in indigenous languages must be part of the equation.

Challenges

Publishing in indigenous languages faces many problems. The history and geography of Africa are significant challenges. All of Sub-Saharan Africa, except Ethiopia, was colonized, and in every case the colonial power imposed its language on the colony. Colonial policies differed, of course, with the British allowing more latitude for local languages than did, for example, the French. The legacy of colonial languages and of the specific policies of the colonizers concerning language development, the languages used for instruction in the schools, and the structure of postsecondary education remains powerful in Africa.

In no colonized territory were indigenous languages strongly supported or publishing encouraged. In Belgian and Portuguese colonies, education was discouraged at all levels, and there was little publishing in any language. The French preferred to publish and print books for their colonies in France. The British had a more laissez faire policy, permitting some publishing in their colonies, but maintaining controls and using publishers in England to publish many school books. The British also relied on private organizations, especially Christian missionary groups, to sponsor both schools and publishing activities.

The use of European languages during the colonial era for administration, education, law, and politics had a powerful impact on national development. In no case was a postcolonial African country prepared to jettison the colonial language at the time of independence. In only a few countries, such as Tanzania, was a significant effort made to foster the use of an African language—in this case, Kiswahili—as a national language with the goal of displacing English.

The colonial powers had many reasons for using their own languages. This policy was certainly most efficient for the colonial administration, and it permitted the intact transfer of the colonizer's legal and administrative systems. European languages also linked the emerging elites in the colonies to the metropole, creating ties that have lasted to the present time in many cases.

The fact that the predominant European languages in Africa are English and French creates special problems for African language publishing. Both are "world languages" and for that reason have considerable attraction. Further, in the era of the Internet and the World Wide Web, English, as the language that dominates electronic communication worldwide, is especially desirable. As African countries are linked to the Internet, there is pressure to maintain the status quo of English and, to a lesser extent, French. The major multinational publishers use English and are interested in expanding their reach. The new technologies in communications and in publishing strengthen the already dominant world languages. The increased concentration of ownership of publishing firms worldwide also poses special problems for indigenous language publishing.

Since the European colonies in Africa were superimposed on traditional political, cultural, religious, and linguistic boundaries, the colonial borders of the colonies, which later became the boundaries of independent African nations, made little linguistic or cultural sense. In almost every colonial territory, a variety of ethnic, linguistic, and cultural traditions coexisted. Many of these had little in common with each other. At the time of independence, new states had to quickly set up political and administrative systems; in most cases, they simply kept the existing colonial patterns. The entrenched status of the colonial language made the use of indigenous languages even more difficult.

Africa's extraordinary linguistic complexity has created special problems for publishing in African languages and for the use of African languages as national languages. Even small countries are multilingual, making the choice of one language as the national one difficult. It is not unusual for the number of languages to be in the hundreds, with each spoken by fairly small populations. Only a few countries have languages spoken by large enough segments of the population to be chosen easily as the national language or to support a viable publishing industry.

In some countries, as noted, the proliferation of languages made it difficult to select one as the national language. In others, large language groups existed, but conflicts over the control of the new nation determined the choice of one language over the others. Nigeria, for example, has both problems. It has a large number of languages within its borders; it also has several languages, Igbo, Hausa, and Yoruba, which are spoken by large segments of the population. Choosing any of these major languages as the national language or the dominant language for education has proven to be politically difficult.

Many languages are spoken by populations extending across several countries, but are dominant in none. This may create cross-border linguistic and political tensions. In theory, regional markets for indigenous language publications may be created, but the practical problems of cross-border trade in many parts of Africa hinder this positive development.

Many African languages did not lend themselves for use as media of publishing and education, having no written scripts, grammatical conventions, or standardized usage. In many cases, European Christian missionaries created the written forms of African languages, generally using the Latin script. In a few other cases, Arabic script was used. Creating written forms for traditional languages makes much more challenging the already complex and expensive process of curriculum development for the schools, as well as publishing for both educational and general purposes.

Throughout most of Africa, the business of politics, trade, government, law, and modern culture is conducted in European languages. Legal systems in these countries function in European languages, not African ones. Even the straightforward task of translating legal documents, historical materials, and the like is a daunting one. Further, the minority of the population literate in the language of power is often not very enthusiastic about giving up its monopoly on the authority associated with literacy in a European language. Only a minority of the population in African countries has been exposed to advanced schooling in the European languages. The numbers able to obtain a postsecondary degree are very small: Africa has the lowest participation rate in higher education of any continent. Higher education is offered exclusively in European languages. The elite remains committed to the continued use of European languages.

Some larger languages, such as Kiswahili, have received government support—with the assistance of professional linguists and lexicographers—to address the complex technical issues involved with language development. Size is also a factor. For many languages, an insufficient number of speakers—and potential readers—exists to make the language viable for publishing. The fact is that without a sufficient number of potential buyers of books, newspapers, magazines, and other published materials, a publishing industry will not be feasible.

Purchasing power is limited for speakers of many African languages, restricting their publishing potential. The number of speakers is important, but equally crucial is the number of speakers who are literate and can afford to buy published materials. Economic power is concentrated in the hands of people who are literate in a European language, and thus preference is often given to these languages. This is true for reasons of prestige and also because there is a much wider choice of materials to buy. Often, buyers who are literate in more than one language will prefer to buy European language books rather than local indigenous language publications, even if the local materials are less expensive. Lack of purchasing power is a central problem for indigenous language publishing: without a market, it is not possible to publish books. But if no books are available in these languages, the market will not emerge because readers will have no choices. Readers, once accustomed to buying European language materials, will seldom choose to buy local language books.

Publishing in Africa has become increasingly privatized. Government publishers and parastatal agencies that were influential in the years following independence in much of Africa have been displaced by private sector publishers. Much of this privatization has taken place as a result of pressure from the World Bank and other international lending agencies, but the fact is that public sector publishing did not work well. Insofar as private sector publishers are able to build up a market for their books, participate in textbook publishing, and obtain access to capital to publish books, this will have a positive impact on indigenous language publishing.

These are some of the issues associated with publishing in indigenous languages in Africa. The problems may seem insurmountable, but considerable progress has been made. It is possible that a discussion of the experiences of other countries with indigenous publishing may have some relevance for thinking about Africa's future.

Comparative Perspectives

While much of the failure in indigenous language publishing in Africa stems from the current economic and political situation, other developing countries have faced similar challenges in creating local publishing industries. In many parts of the world, minority languages are undervalued or ignored by publishers, governments, and the educational system. For example, in Peru and Bolivia significant minorities of indigenous peoples use languages such as Quechua. Very little publishing occurs in these languages. For the most part, schooling takes place in Spanish. This situation has contributed to the historic marginalization of these indigenous populations.

Language is a politically sensitive issue in many parts of the world. The conflict between French-speaking Quebec and the rest of Canada still threatens the unity of the country. Disagreements between French and Flemish speakers in Belgium remain a central fact of the nation's political life. Conflicts over both language and ethnicity remain volatile and intense, occasionally spilling over into violence, for example, in Spain between the Spanish-speaking majority and the Catalans and Basques in the north. Similar conflicts can be seen in Sri Lanka. Language groups try to protect language rights, and books and publishing are often part of the conflict. Along with the revival of nationalism, even Scotland has seen a modest resurgence of support for the Scottish language. Israel succeeded in reviving Hebrew, turning it into the language of modern government and education. Many have insisted on a link between nation building, ethnic identity, and language. This insistence has led to conflict and acrimony. But as these examples show, language has also been a force contributing to national identity. The issues involved affect both developing and industrialized nations.

Indonesia is an example of a developing country that successfully adopted a national language policy that both displaced the colonial language (Dutch) and imposed an indigenous language on a multilingual and ethnically diverse nation with a population of more than 180 million. At the time of the struggle for independence in 1949, nationalist leaders decided to jettison Dutch and adopt a language commonly used in the region—but not the mother tongue of the major population group, the Malays—as the national language. This language, *Bahasa Indonesia*, or national Indonesian language, became the language of government and education at all levels. Books were written and published in *Bahasa Indonesia*. A greater challenge was the provision of textbooks and related materials for the postsecondary sectors. Basic university-level textbooks were, after some delays, published. With more than 1.5 million students in postsecondary education, the Indonesian market for books was large. A general publishing industry in *Bahasa Indonesia* gradually emerged, as well. Early governmental insistence on the use of a common indigenous language permitted Indonesia to focus its linguistic energies.

It is significant that the language chosen was not the language of the majority of the population, Javanese, but rather a fairly unthreatening language linked linguistically to most of the languages and dialects spoken in the country. Government funds were provided to build up the language, to translate, prepare, and publish original texts. Indonesia had several advantages: its colonial language, Dutch, was not a world language; virtually all of its indigenous languages and dialects shared common linguistic roots; a decision was made to use the Latin script; and a strong nationalist movement that stressed linguistic unity as part of its program took and held power during the first several decades after independence.

India, in contrast, has faced more formidable linguistic challenges. The leaders of India's nationalist movement, most notably Mohandas Gandhi, supported the use of Hindi, the mother tongue of about 45 percent of India's population, as the national language. This aroused resentment and opposition from other linguistic groups, especially those in the south. The southern languages, such as Tamil and Telugu, have completely different linguistic roots from Hindi, and are written in a different script. The Indian constitution lists 15 officially recognized languages, including English. Hindi is the national language, with English the officially recognized associate national language until such time as all of the regions agree that English should be dropped. There are also hundreds of smaller languages and dialects. A half-century after independence, English remains prominent at the national level, and has perhaps even entrenched its position. For example, while most schoolchildren are educated in their mother tongues, the elite sends its children to English-medium private schools. Some of the universities, including most of the prestigious ones, continue to use English as the main language of instruction and examination. The central government operates in Hindi and English. The states use their own languages, usually in addition to English, as well.

The publishing industry is equally complicated in this country of almost 1 billion people. Close to half of the books published in India are in English, although only about 5 percent of the population is literate in English. Purchasing power for books in English far exceeds that for the other languages, and English language books are the only ones that receive national distribution. Despite the problems, many of the indigenous languages—such as Bengali, Marathi, Tamil, and, of course, Hindi—support active publishing industries. The fact that there are 55 million Marathi speakers, for example, permits the growth of local publishing industries alongside English language publishing.

Smaller developing countries have painstakingly managed to build up indigenous language publishing, as well. Countries such as Laos and Cambodia, in Southeast Asia, publish books and run their educational systems in their main indigenous languages. Publishing in their languages, Lao and Khmer, which have established scripts, is poorly developed. Books for schools are prepared by government agencies, which are often unable to adequately supply needed books. Laos and Cambodia remain firmly committed to their national languages, despite poor economic conditions and small markets.

To be sure, examples of successful indigenous language publishing can be found in Africa. For example, the famous "chap books" in the Igbo language of Nigeria are a notable success story. These slim short fiction and self-help volumes helped to get Igbo language publishing started and raised consciousness of books among the population. The success of the undertaking was based on careful attention to the potential market for specific types of books. Publishers also relied on local authors and took advantage of nontraditional distribution channels, such as local markets. Most of those involved in producing books in the early days were small entrepreneurs. Both literacy levels and purchasing power among the Igbo are relatively high, so a market exists for books. The chap books filled a particular market niche not occupied by other books or magazines and paved the way for a more diversified publishing enterprise.

These examples, although anecdotal, are intended to offer comparisons with the experience of a few other countries in the development of publishing in indigenous languages. Some countries have moved decisively to foster indigenous language publishing link the educational system to an emerging publishing industry so that textbook markets could help support other kinds of publishing.

Next Steps

While it is not possible to present a blueprint for fostering African language publishing, there are central elements that must be considered.

Economic Viability

African publishing generally lacks capital. Credit is difficult for publishers to obtain. Publishing has a modest margin of profitability and a slow rate of return worldwide. Indigenous language publishing has to contend with limited markets and purchasing power, as well as low literacy rates. On the positive side, publishing requires relatively little capital. Revolving loan programs, special credit arrangements with banks, and support for African language publishing by established publishers can all contribute to an economic base for African language publishing. Indigenous language publishing can often be undertaken by very small enterprises that make use of small-scale printers, binders, and others in the "book chain." Indeed, books can sometimes be produced by stationery shops, school book distributors, and others who have publishing as a sideline.

MARKETING AND MARKET RESEARCH

The fact is that not all African languages have the potential for successful publishing. Informal research is needed concerning market needs, size, and related factors. Realistically assessing the practical viability for publishing is essential. Books need to be effectively marketed, which requires going beyond traditional sales channels, such as bookshops. There are not enough bookshops, especially in rural areas. Using traditional African market structures has been effective in Nigeria and elsewhere. Innovative strategies are essential.

REGIONAL MARKETS

For many African languages, the community of readers spreads across national borders. Taking advantage of regional markets, although difficult in the current African situation, is often necessary. Copublishing in linguistic areas that are separated by political boundaries may be a way of distributing books across national borders.

LANGUAGE RESEARCH AND DEVELOPMENT

The process of language development needs to be part of a growing market for books in many of the smaller African languages. Formalizing grammar, spelling, and other elements of the language is necessary for a successful book industry in the long run. University-based linguists can assist publishers and government experts in systematizing African languages.

Conclusion

Without question, most of Africa faces severe difficulties in the development of indigenous language publishing. Compared to much of the rest of the developing world, Africa has more unfavorable economic and political circumstances at the present time. The linguistic situation is especially complex, and many African languages have too few speakers to support a viable publishing industry. Purchasing power, even in languages with sufficiently numerous speakers, is generally limited. Many languages were not used for written communication and have no standard script or grammatical structure.

Perhaps daunted by these problems, African governments have been less committed to the development of indigenous languages than governments in Asia. Despite the obstacles, the need for books in African languages is important, both for the expansion and maintenance of literacy and for the emergence and sustenance of culture and civil society.

2

Publishing in Kiswahili: A Writer's Perspective

M.M. Mulokozi

Introduction

This chapter discusses the problems and issues of publishing in Kiswahili from a writer's point of view. I begin with a brief historical survey of the development of Kiswahili in East Africa. This is then followed by a historical review of publishing in Kiswahili in Kenya and Tanzania and an examination of the general socio-political context in which it takes place.[1] The final part of this essay will analyze the problems of publishing in Kiswahili pertaining to each stage in the book chain, i.e. authorship, publishing, book distribution/and sales, and readership. Printing is not discussed because it is beyond the scope of the chapter. At each stage of the discussion, pertinent propositions for remedial action will be made whenever appropriate.

Kiswahili Language

Kiswahili—or Swahili, as it is sometimes called in English—is currently the leading indigenous African language. It is spoken or understood by about 100 million people in Eastern and Central Africa and in parts of the Middle East. Kiswahili is the official national language of Kenya, Tanzania, and Uganda, and one of the national languages of Congo (Zaire). The majority of the speakers of Kiswahili are concentrated in these countries, though many Kiswahili speakers are also found in other nearby countries, especially Burundi, Mozambique, Rwanda, Somalia, and Zambia.

Linguistically, Kiswahili is a Bantu language that evolved along the East Coast of Africa, and through time assimilated many words from Arabic, Persian, Turkish, Portuguese, and Indian languages. In recent years, Kiswahili has borrowed extensively from English. In the nineteenth century, Kiswahili spread quickly inland as a commercial *lingua franca*.[2] Toward the end of the century, the German colonial rulers of what is now mainland Tanzania adopted Kiswahili, for pragmatic reasons, as the language of the lower levels of administration and education, confining German to higher levels. This policy ensured the spread and consolidation of Kiswahili throughout the country, and was to have an abiding impact on Tanzania's language situation. The British, who took over the colonial administration after the defeat of the Germans in World War I, continued the German language policy of using Kiswahili whenever convenient, but replaced the German language with English, in the higher levels of government and education. In Kenya and Uganda, the British, who were the colonial power, adopted Kiswahili as a *lingua franca* and a language of administration and of the military. They also attempted, with varying degrees of success, to spread the language among the populace through the school system and, to a lesser extent, the Christian missions. They faced, however, much resistance from both the missionaries and the larger nationalities, such as the Baganda in Uganda, whose languages were already serving as de facto *lingua francae* in their "spheres of influence."

The most controversial, and arguably the most important, legacy of the British was the standardization of Kiswahili, carried out through the Inter-Territorial Language Committee for East African Dependencies—later to become the East African Swahili Committee—which was established in 1930. After the first wave of African independence in the early 1960s, the new politics of nationalism, pan-Africanism, African liberation, and Ujamaa aroused greater interest in Kiswahili as an expression of African identity and culture and as the future replacement of English in most spheres of national life. Accordingly, Kiswahili was declared the national language of Tanzania in 1962, Uganda in 1973, and Kenya in 1977. It was this increasing importance of Kiswahili in the life of the people of East Africa that created the need for publishing in Kiswahili.

Throughout the colonial period, German, and later British, government officials, missionaries, and scholars compiled grammars, glossaries, and dictionaries; translated biblical tracts and hymn books; translated and wrote secular books for use in schools; transcribed, translated, and published classical Kiswahili literature; and edited magazines in and on Kiswahili. In the process, they turned Kiswahili into the leading language of publishing in East Africa.

Development of Publishing in Kiswahili

Publishing in East Africa began in the nineteenth century as part of the missionary enterprise; it was originally inseparable from printing. In 1887, the Church Missionary Society founded the Ndia Kuu Press at Freretown in Mombasa, Kenya. In Tanzania, the Universities Mission to Central Africa Press was set up in Zanzibar in 1875. Other mission presses, Taveta in 1890 and Magila in 1905, were also established. At about the same time, the colonial governments—the British in Zanzibar and the Germans in the Tanzanian mainland—started their own government presses. A number of Kiswahili magazines were established by Christian missions before 1910 in both Kenya and Tanzania.[3] Then, in 1923, the British in then Tanganyika founded *Mambo Leo*, a news-*cum*-literary magazine that survived until the 1950s and was the main vehicle for budding Kiswahili writers of the colonial period.

Until about 1950, almost all publishing of Kiswahili books was for school use. The books were usually published outside the country, especially in South Africa and Britain. Then, in 1948, the British set up the East African Literature Bureau (EALB) to serve as the local publisher for primary school textbooks and other books in African languages and English. (A complete list of acronyms appears at the end of this chapter.) The headquarters of EALB was in Nairobi, Kenya. It had branches in Dar es Salaam, Tanzania, and Kampala, Uganda. In addition to publishing books, the EALB also ran public libraries, including a mobile library service.

The EALB did so well that it had published more than 1,000 titles in 16 different languages by the early 1960s. Some of the best East African fiction writers and poets of the 1950s and 1960s were published by the Bureau. Unfortunately, contrary to normal practice, EALB's best-selling titles were usually handed over to private British publishers after the first edition, thereby reducing the EALB's ability to expand.

In addition to the EALB, a number of British publishers, notably Longman, Oxford, Nelson, Heinemann, Evans Brothers, Macmillan, Cambridge University Press, McGraw Hill, Collins, and Pitman opened offices in Nairobi in the 1950s and 1960s. After independence, some of these also opened offices in Dar es Salaam and Kampala, mainly as marketing outlets.

In the 1960s, local commercial and noncommercial publishers also came into being. These included the Institute of Kiswahili Research based at the then University College of Dar es Salaam (1964[4]); Jomo Kenyatta Foundation (JKF) (Nairobi, 1965), a parastatal; East African Publishing House (EAPH) (Nairobi, Dar es Salaam, and Kampala, 1965), which was owned by the East African Cultural Trust; Equatorial Publishers (Kenya, 1965); and the Tanzania Publishing House (TPH), a parastatal founded in 1966. In the 1970s, more local publishers appeared: among those, in Kenya were Comb Books, Transafrica Publishers and Book Distributors, Foundation Books, Njogu Gitene Publications, Shungwaya Books, Bookwise, Migi Teki, Gazelle Books; and in Tanzania, Black Star Agency, Meza Publications, Tausi Publishers, Continental Publishers, Jomssi Publishers, and the Dar es Salaam University Press (founded in 1979). The break-up of the East African Community (EAC) in 1976 contributed directly to the collapse of the EALB in 1977 and indirectly to the collapse of the EAPH in 1987.

Indigenous private publishing companies became quite numerous in the 1970s and 1980s. Today, more than 130 publishers are registered in Kenya,[5] and 150 in Tanzania.[6] The leading publishers in Kenya are: JKF, Kenya Literature Bureau (KLB), Longhorn, Oxford University Press (OUP), East African Educational Publishers (EAEP), Phoenix, and Lake Publishers. In Tanzania the leading publishers are: TPH, Eastern Africa Publications Ltd. (EAPL),[7] Dar es Salaam University Press, Ben and Company, Press and Publicity Centre, OUP, Ndanda-Peramiho Mission Press, Mkuki na Nyota, and Heko publishers. There are several other up-and-coming Tanzanian publishers, such as the Kagera Writers Cooperative, Diamond Publishers, Mture Publications, and E & D Publications. The first two started with much enthusiasm in 1987 and 1991 respectively, but today appear to have lost momentum.

Briefly, the development of publishing in East Africa from the beginning was driven by government policies and actions. Even after independence, the actions of the governments, such as the "free enterprise" policies in Kenya, the Ujamaa policies in Tanzania, the break-up of the EAC, and the divergent language and educational policies in the East African states influenced the development of publishing activities in the member states and, to a great extent, defined the problems and issues faced by the industry.

Current Problems and Issues

The problems and issues facing publishing in Kiswahili may be understood best through a review of the problems besetting the various stages and components of the book chain from the creator of the book, the author, to its consumer, the reader. These will now be addressed in the context of the overall government policies and socio-political situation in Kenya and Tanzania.

Economic and Cultural Situation

In discussing the problems of publishing in East Africa, it is important to bear in mind the fact that we are dealing with a largely oral society. This is especially the case in the rural areas, where most of the people live. In the majority of rural households, and in a good number of urban ones, reading and writing occurs very rarely, if at all. Indeed, for most people who are able to read, the only reading materials they have regular access to are religious scriptures and hymns—whether Christian or Islamic. Thus, although the literacy rates are said to be high, at least in Tanzania, which in the early 1980s claimed a literacy rate of more than 90 percent, the reading rate is still very low. Coupled with this is the low economic level: the annual per capita income of East Africans ranges between US $120 and $350. Hence, even if the people were literate, most of them could certainly not afford to buy books on a regular basis, if at all. It is this poverty-stricken and semi-literate social base that is expected to support the publishing industry.

LANGUAGE POLICY

A conducive language policy is the precondition for successful publishing in Kiswahili and, for that matter, any other language. In the East African context, the policies of colonial governments had a decisive influence on publishing in Kiswahili. The British policy of encouraging the use of Kiswahili in the lower levels of education and administration, especially in Kenya and Tanzania, gave impetus to and defined the nature of publishing in Kiswahili during the colonial period. Kiswahili publishing was primarily intended to meet school needs for textbooks and supplementary readers and, to a lesser extent, to meet the needs of adult literacy. Not surprisingly, publishing of general literature not required for school use was not encouraged. In Uganda, where Kiswahili was not allowed to take root, publishing in the language has not flourished.

As independence approached, the British colonial government in Kenya changed its policy regarding Kiswahili; it started to discourage its teaching and use in schools for fear that it might serve as a uniting factor for Africans during the Mau Mau war. This decision retarded the spread of Kiswahili in Kenya for almost 20 years, until a new policy came into force during the Daniel Arap-Moi era.

In 1975, the Kenyan government began to emphasize the teaching of Kiswahili as a symbol of national unity and identity. It directed that Kiswahili should be a compulsory subject in Kenyan secondary schools.[8] This policy had a marked impact on the spread of Kiswahili in Kenya, and hence on Kiswahili publishing. More books were written and published for use in the school system and to cater to the new ex-secondary school readership. Publishing of Kiswahili books flourished as never before.

In Tanzania, the colonial policy on Kiswahili remained in force until independence. After independence, the nationalist government declared Kiswahili the official national language and created a number of organs for its promotion. As a result, Kiswahili use grew very quickly in Tanzania, along with publishing in Kiswahili. This led Walter Bgoya to remark rightly that Kiswahili is the only language that makes publishing possible in Tanzania.[9]

In at least one area of publishing—textbooks—language policy in both Kenya and Tanzania has had a negative impact. In Kenya, Kiswahili was abandoned as a medium of primary education in most schools in the early 1950s, and has not been reinstated to date, except for some schools along the coast and in large urban areas. This politically inspired decision has meant that no books on any school subject—except language and literature—are being written or published in Kiswahili. This policy effectively confines Kiswahili publishing in Kenya to general books and bars it from rigorous academic spheres. This in turn reinforces the idea that Kiswahili is only a language of the streets, political rallies, and the market place.

In Tanzania, Kiswahili has been a medium of primary education—up to Standard VI—since colonial times. It became the sole medium of primary education after 1967. In secondary schools, until recently, Kiswahili was used to teach political education, Kiswahili language and literature, and sometimes religious studies. All other subjects were taught in English. The result of this policy was a mushrooming of Kiswahili language textbooks and supplementary readers for all primary school subjects, and a dearth of such material for higher levels. In 1987, the ministry then responsible for culture commissioned translation into Kiswahili of school textbooks for biology, chemistry, physics, mathematics, geography, history, and bookkeeping. To date, those manuscripts have not been published, mainly because the medium of education in secondary schools is still English. The new cultural policy unveiled in 1997 states that English will be the medium of instruction in secondary and higher education—but it does not say when. That statement alone has already sent publishers rushing to the Ministry of Education and Culture (MEC) begging to be allowed to publish the Kiswahili translations. Obviously, if the MEC implements this decision, publishing in Kiswahili will receive a major boost.

POLITICAL, ECONOMIC, AND EDUCATIONAL POLICIES

Aside from language policies, other policy factors that determined or influenced the course of publishing of Kiswahili books were economic and educational policies, especially those related to textbook provision. In Kenya, unbridled capitalism has been the dominant policy throughout the independence period. This has meant that the multinational publishing houses were never disturbed, and continued to provide, whether through imports or local publishing, the bulk of Kenya's general and higher education book needs. Likewise, the printing infrastructure and the bookshops and distribution channels remained more or less intact, thus ensuring that the private sector continued to play a major role in the book chain. As regards the supply of primary and secondary school textbooks, however, the Kenyan government created four state monopolies: JKF (1966), Kenya Institute of Education (KIE, 1968), Kenya School Equipment Scheme (KSES, 1970), and the KLB (1977) for the purpose. The KIE prepared curricula and wrote textbook manuscripts, while JKF and KLB concentrated on publishing. The KSES distributed materials to the schools.[10] Nevertheless, these institutions were unable to meet all the textbook needs of the school system; hence, the multinational publishers still retained a big share of the textbook market. The result of this policy was that indigenous private publishing did not flourish, especially after the collapse of EALB and EAPH, which fell victim to the contradictions between the Kenyan "private enterprise" bourgeoisie and its state-based rivals in Tanzania and, to a lesser extent, Uganda. In such a situation, publishing of general Kiswahili books could hardly receive priority, except when they were meant for school use.

In Tanzania, at the height of Ujamaa politics in the late 1960s and early 1970s, nationalization of private enterprises led to the creation of state monopolies in book writing, publishing, and distribution, notably the Tanzania Institute of Education, TPH, EAPL (a successor to EALB), Tanzania Elimu Supplies (a textbook distribution monopoly), and, in the printing sub-sector, Printpak Tanzania and the National Printing Company Ltd. As a result of the confinement of textbook production and distribution to these state monopolies, private publishers and booksellers, including multinational publishers, lost business and most of them closed or changed their business lines. The multinationals, especially Macmillan and Longman, actually decided to withdraw from Tanzania altogether. OUP remained only as a nominal outlet for materials produced in Kenya and the United Kingdom. The unintended result of this was the collapse of the Tanzanian publishing industry, and hence of publishing in Kiswahili. Thus, only about 77 creative literature titles, mostly in Kiswahili, were produced in Tanzania by the secular publishers between 1985 and 1995. That works out to an average of under eight titles per year.[11] Efforts to revive the industry began in the late 1980s and have continued to the present time. These efforts will be discussed later in this chapter.

The Kiswahili Writer in the Book Chain

There is no reliable data on the number of Kiswahili writers, but I estimate that published *book* writers using Kiswahili in Kenya and Tanzania number more than 3,000, if writers of both creative and nonfiction literature are included. To this list we may add the numerous poets[12] and short story writers who publish in newspapers and magazines,[13] and the many playwrights who stage plays that are not published in book form. In all, when we talk about Kiswahili authors in Kenya and Tanzania, we are referring to a growing community of more than 10,000 individuals. These are the people whose problems are addressed in this section. There is no doubt that they constitute the biggest number of individual stakeholders in the book sector.

These authors are the basis of the publishing industry: publishers cannot exist without authors, though authors can and do exist without publishers. In theory, authors should receive recognition and priority in book development policies and practices. In reality, however, they are the group most ignored by both publishers and governments.

Many of the problems facing writers in general apply to writers in Kiswahili. Nevertheless, because of the language factor, there are other problems that are specific to Kiswahili writing and publishing. This section will identify and discuss the general and specific problems facing writing and publishing in Kiswahili, within the framework of the book chain.

A short listing of the problems faced by Kiswahili writers at each stage of the book chain includes the following: poor writing skills, poor author-publisher relations, lack of motivation, publishing problems, readership and distribution problems, copyright problems, censorship, and organizational and coordination problems.

Poor Writing Skills

Most editors and writers tell us that manuscripts submitted to publishers are generally poorly written and poorly organized, even when they contain important and valuable content. This is the case regardless of the language in which a given work is written, though, in Tanzania at least, the problem is more serious in works written in English. This is partly a result of the lack of training and exposure to good literature among newer writers. Most Kiswahili writers are self-taught. No schools currently exist for Kiswahili writers, although some university departments in Kenya and Tanzania teach certain aspects of creative writing. Unfortunately, such courses are rarely fully fledged or comprehensive.

Writing as such is not taught in schools either. The only "training" most writers ever receive is through the *ad hoc* and irregular workshops organized by writers and publishers associations that are funded by donor agencies. The exception is the regular training carried out in Tanzania in the last seven years under the auspices of the Children's Book Project (CBP), in cooperation with the writers' associations. These workshops have proved to be invaluable to the authors, and quite a few promising writers have emerged from them.

Since such courses and workshops are donor-funded, writers and publishers have to adopt a long-term perspective and strategy that can be implemented even when the donors have left. Such a perspective should ensure that writing skills are made part of the normal school and college curricula and that professional training for writers and editors should be introduced in university and college curricula. Furthermore, literature-promotion activities, such as writing clubs and school magazines, including "wall magazines," need to be re-introduced in schools and colleges.

AUTHOR-PUBLISHER RELATIONS

For publishing to succeed, author-publisher relations should be a partnership rather than a beggar-versus-benefactor relationship. It should be built on mutual trust and scrupulous honesty. Unfortunately, this is rarely the case in East Africa. On the contrary, author-publisher relations have generally been characterized by dishonesty and unethical practices, including outright cheating and swindling.

During colonial times, contrary to normal practice in Europe, British publishers of Kiswahili literature written by "natives" did not treat the African writers as partners with the same rights as European writers. More often than not, they tricked them into "selling" their manuscripts at the lowest possible price, after which the authors had no other rights whatsoever to their works.[14] A few examples will illustrate this exploitive relationship.

In the early 1930s, the Kenyan writer, James Juma Mbotela (c. 1888–1976) of Mombasa, arguably the first East African novelist, entered and won a prize in a British essay/story writing competition. He was awarded £5 for his Kiswahili manuscript. Some missionaries and a British publisher became interested in the work. They persuaded him to "sell" it to the publisher at the give away price of 100 Shillings. In 1934, the book was published as the novel *Uhuru wa Watumwa*, and became a bestseller at once. It became a school reader throughout East Africa, was translated into English, and has been on the school list ever since. Mbotela died a poor man in 1976, while his British publishers were—and still are—making millions from his work. In his memoirs, Mbotela complained bitterly:

> Now I realize that the book has been reprinted many times in Swahili and English and is much in use in Kenya and Tanzania; but I have not received any of the royalties. That's not right. You

> see, the African was taught not to worry much about material things; but the European missionaries were always thinking about security and they used the Africans. Anyway, I believe I have made a contribution by writing this book.[15]

In the early 1970s, Mbotela revised the book, hoping to issue another—and probably better—edition, but:

> the book had been published and successfully sold in Swahili and English versions, and since Mbotela had initially received a flat sum of five pounds for the publication rights in 1934, the publishers were not interested in altering that situation, which would have allowed Mbotela to share in the royalties.[16]

The case of Shaaban Robert (1909–1962), East Africa's foremost writer of the colonial period, is also telling. Less than a half of his 22 works were published in his lifetime, largely because he could not find honest publishers. In his autobiography, *Maisha Yangu na Baada ya Miaka Hamsini*, Robert described his unethical treatment at the hands of British publishers:

> In 1951, I was paid only Sh. 200 for a work that put an income of about Sh. 10,000 for 5,000 copies into the pockets of others, with the possibility of many future reprints. My agreement with the publishers was for a lump sum payment. . . . As if I had been a donkey or the most abject fool, I was, in 1959, asked to offer yet another work for a promise of a 5 percent royalty whose calculation was the publisher's guarded secret. When I refused, a pretext was found to reject my works—I was told that no publisher will be able to publish my works without a guarantor. Nor was this an idle threat: after only a few days, one of my works which was with a European publisher was returned to me, and some of the publishers based in East Africa turned against me. . . .
> In 1954, I was not paid a single copper cent for a work that could bring in Sh. 25,000 for 5,000 copies. My agreement with the publishers was to share the costs and the profits equally. . . . When I wrote to claim my share . . . in 1960, I was paid only 800 [Shillings].[17]

Robert tried to evade these racketeers by publishing some of his works with Witwatersrand Press in South Africa, but here again distance was a major handicap. Eventually, in 1959, he set up his own company, Tanga Art and Literature, but unfortunately did not live long enough to see it prosper.

A more recent case relates to the collapse of the former EAPH in 1987. This company was set up in suspicious circumstances in 1965 by a Non-Governmental Organization (NGO) known as the East African Cultural Trust, and soon became a leading publisher of general books in English, Kiswahili, and other local languages. The EAPH fell victim to the collapse of the East African Community when the closure of the Kenya-Tanzania border in the late 1970s made it difficult for the EAPH Board of Directors to meet and for its publications to be disseminated throughout East Africa, which it had been able to do previously. Amidst these uncertainties, some members of the Board and management in Nairobi seized the opportunity to plunder the company, thus causing its liquidation in 1987. Hundreds of titles, including some by such distinguished authors as Okot p'Bitek, Ayi Kwei Armah, Julius Nyerere, Jared Angira, John Ruganda, Ebrahim Hussein, E. Kezilahabi, and Penina Muhando, perished with the company. Even before the bankruptcy, authors were not paid their royalties regularly, if at all. I was one of these EAPH authors, and hardly received a cent in royalties for my book, *Mukwava wa Uhehe*, which was being used as a Kiswahili literature textbook in all Kenyan secondary schools. Even when the company was put into receivership, authors were not included among the claimants who were to be paid from the proceeds of the sale of EAPH assets.

The above cases are not isolated. They reflect a "normal" trend in East African publishing. That much every writer knows. Among the current 100 or so active publishers operating in East Africa, very few—maybe less than 20—are above board.

At the moment, the Tanzanian government is in the process of divesting itself from commercial activities, in line with World Bank directives. Its two main parastatal publishers, EAPL (formerly the Tanzania branch of the defunct EALB) and TPH, are apparently being offered for sale. The Dar es Salaam University Press may soon also follow suit.

EAPL has some fixed assets that it inherited from the former EALB. It also has old stocks and back titles going back to 1948. TPH has no fixed assets, but like EAPL it has old stocks and back titles that have been selling quite well. Obviously, it is these old stocks and titles that are being offered for sale. Yet, surprisingly, the authors, who legally own or co-own the titles and stock, have not been consulted, nor have they been invited to participate in the transactions or buy shares in the companies. Thus, the authors' books and rights are being offered to the highest (or lowest) bidder without their knowledge or consent.

A recent seminar on author-publisher relations reflects the growing interest to address this problem. A number of leading African writers and publishers attended the 1998 seminar, held in Tanzania. All the parties agreed that a new beginning, a new deal, and a new code of ethics be put in place. It was, therefore, decided that the publishers and writers in each country should work out a code of conduct that would spell out clearly the rights, duties, and obligations of each party.[18]

Lack of Motivation

Kiswahili authors are not motivated to write books because they are not sure of getting published; and, even when published, they are not sure they would be paid their royalties. Many leading authors lost thousands of shillings when the EAPH and EALB were disbanded. The present privatization drive in Tanzania does not seem to favor writers either; the future of the parastatal publishers such as TPH and EAPL is still uncertain, as is the future of the hundreds of works published by them. On their part, the smaller private publishers are barely able to survive, cannot reach the potential market, and are often unable, unwilling, or too dishonest to pay royalties.

One way of motivating authors is to offer literary awards for good writing. Unfortunately, no such literary awards exist for Kiswahili writers, with the possible exception of the Noma Prize.[19] Otherwise, literary prizes are usually offered to authors writing in European languages.[20] Attempts by the National Kiswahili Council in Tanzania to offer prizes to the best Kiswahili writers in 1995 floundered when the people in charge decided that awarding Kiswahili writers was a lesser priority than, say, paying per diems and setting allowances to unproductive and unpoetic bureaucrats.

Under these circumstances, the task of motivating Kiswahili authors should be undertaken by the Kiswahili publishers and writers' associations. Kiswahili publishers and writers should institute ways and means of motivating and recognizing good writers, for example, by offering annual or periodic national literature and publishing awards, introducing annual or periodic writing competitions for budding writers, including school pupils, and creating a mechanism to ensure the purchase of a given number of copies of each locally published book for public use, such as public libraries and schools. While these measures would be welcome, in the final analysis, the most important and more lasting motivation for any writer is to be published, read, and remunerated accordingly. Naturally, the onus for ensuring this lies with the publishers.

Publishing Problems

The publishing problems facing the Kiswahili writer today may be simply summarized as shortage of reliable publishing outlets. This shortage cannot be separated from the problems facing the publishing industry as a whole, for the publishers are the author's partners through which a literary work sees the light of day. If for some reason the publishers cannot play their part, the whole process of making books available to people collapses. This is in essence what has happened in Tanzania and Uganda in the last 20 years. In Kenya, thanks to a different set of circumstances, there was a decline rather than a collapse of publishing. We shall now examine briefly the Tanzanian and Kenyan experiences.

Tanzanian publishers have been facing problems of a political-economic nature. First, the break-up of the East African Community in 1977 had catastrophic consequences for companies such as the EALB and EAPH that had East African operations. Second, the collapse of the Tanzanian economy following the Kagera War of 1978-1979 adversely affected the publishing industry. The situation was exacerbated by the then-government policy on textbook writing, production, and distribution, which confined all the operations to parastatal organizations, notably the Institute of Education, the parastatal publishers (TPH and EAPL), and Tanzania Elimu Supplies (TES). This policy effectively killed publishing and the book trade; private publishers could not enter the lucrative school market, and bookshops closed down because they had no books to sell and no reliable market existed outside the school system. By 1985, the publishing industry had all but collapsed.

Thus, although there are more than 150 registered publishers in Tanzania today—among which 54 are members of the Publishers' Association of Tanzania (PATA) 40 of which are still active[21]—publishing outlets for writers are still inadequate. Indeed, only about 77 titles of creative literature were published in Tanzania between 1985 and 1995—an average of less than 8 titles per year.[22]

A PATA report listed five specific problems faced by Tanzanian publishers. These are lack of working capital, lack of credit facilities, lack of market outlets, inability to undertake promotional and marketing activities, and lack of qualified personnel.[23]

These problems, coupled with the aforementioned ill-advised government "confinement" policy, culminated in the collapse of the Tanzanian publishing industry in the 1980s. Consequently, there remained too few able publishers to cater to Tanzanian writers. A few writers opted for self-publishing; but they soon realized that it was not that easy. Most writers, however, either stopped writing or simply locked away their manuscripts in cupboards. In the 1990s, some of these have found outlets in the mushrooming Kiswahili press.

These problems are now being addressed by the government, stakeholders, and donor agencies through deconfinement and commercialization of textbook production and distribution; privatization of publishing parastatals; donor-assisted schemes—such as the CBP, Pilot Project for Publishing, Primary Education Program, and World Bank support; tax rebates on paper; and attempts to create credit facilities for publishers, such as loan-guarantee schemes and equity capital. Of these measures, the most successful so far, in terms of impacting all levels of the book chain, is CBP.

In 1990, the Canadian Organization for Development through Education (CODE) commissioned a consultant, Douglas Pearce, to study the state of book provision for children in Tanzania and advise CODE about what to do. Pearce discovered that there was hardly any publishing of children's books taking place. The few books available were mostly imported and were in English—a language with which most Tanzanian children were not familiar. As Mabala and Kasembe were to write later:

> The sorry situation is reflected also in the children's section of the National Library Services. In 1988, they boasted of 4,000 Junior Non-Fiction and 5,300 Junior Fiction titles. However, of these, only 500 were in Kiswahili (300 Nonfiction and 200 Fiction).[24]

Pearce advised CODE to set up a CBP.[25] The project was duly established in 1991, with the objective of supporting the production and sale of children's books in Tanzania. Soon after, other donors joined in. It became one of the most successful donor-aided book projects in Tanzania. By 1995, the CBP had published 84 titles, organized two children's book fairs, participated in local and international book fairs, and carried out more than 30 training courses for writers, editors, book designers, and artists. Under this scheme, during the first phase of the project that ended in 1996, the publisher of a selected manuscript was required to print at least 5,000 copies. The CBP bought 3,000 copies on the spot, and the publisher was expected to sell the rest. The copies bought by the CBP were distributed to primary schools and libraries in the southern regions of Tanzania.

During the second phase (1996–2001), in addition to the original Phase One objectives and activities, the CBP has a program of promoting readership throughout the country. In this phase, the publisher is required to produce 7,000 copies of the selected title, the CBP buys 5,000 for distribution to selected schools throughout the country, and the publisher is expected to sell the remaining 2,000 copies on the open market.

In addition to making available more than 130 titles for children—mostly in Kiswahili—the CBP has stimulated general publishing by offering selected titles to publishers a ready market for their books and thereby alleviating the problem of publishing capital. Moreover, the CBP has helped raise writing and publishing skills and standards in the country. The CBP was not intended to support the publishing of general or creative literary works for adults, though writers and publishers of such works have benefited indirectly through CBP courses and book fairs, as well as the general stimulation of publishing activities arising out of its programs.

In Kenya, the book publishing policies pursued by the Kenya African National Union (KANU) regime that has ruled the country since independence remained essentially the same as those of the colonial regime. The multinational publishers were allowed to maintain their stronghold, if not strangle hold, on the industry while gradual "Kenyanizing" was encouraged. This put indigenous private publishers at a disadvantage, as they had to compete with long-established and well-financed multinationals. As already shown above, the Kenyan government attempted to correct this imbalance by setting up a number of parastatals, namely JKF, KIE, KSES, and KLB, and charging them with the task of developing and publishing textbooks for schools. This confinement policy disrupted the book trade in Kenya, though not to the same extent as in Tanzania, partly because the book distribution channels (bookshops) were less affected.

In the 1980s, some of the big multinationals, such as Longman and Heinemann, were bought out and indigenized, becoming Longhorn and EAEP respectively. At the same time, many of the remaining multinationals, such as OUP, felt it necessary to at least Kenyanize their managements. In the meantime, more indigenous publishers appeared on the scene; some, such as Shungwaya and Foundation Books, appear to have died in their infancy, while others, such as Phoenix, Focus, and Lake Publishers, are still struggling along. Many of these indigenous publishers publish in both Kiswahili and English. Some, such as EAEP, have indicated that their Kiswahili titles are their major income earner.[26]

The biggest problem faced by Kenyan indigenous publishers is shortage of capital. Banks refuse to lend money to publishing companies because they do not consider publishing to be a profitable or sufficiently viable investment. Following a meeting of African publishers held in Arusha in 1984 during which the problem of capital was discussed, it was agreed that the DHF should establish a loan-guarantee scheme to enable indigenous African publishers to receive bank loans. This scheme was introduced in Kenya in 1988 and enabled some of the indigenous publishers to keep afloat and even expand production. Under this scheme, operated through local banks, the maximum guaranteed loan is about US $41,000. Without this scheme, many of the small Kenyan publishers would have been forced out of business.[27]

For the writer, the advantage of having indigenous publishers is that they are likely to devote some resources to development of local capacity in writing and publishing both out of self-interest and as a matter of national pride. Hence, the indigenous publisher contributes to the development of national literature. But, there are two disadvantages to this approach. First, owing to lack of capital and the requisite skills, and sometimes outright dishonesty, the indigenous publisher sometimes cannot meet the expectations of the author in terms of professional advice and timely production of his/her work, and there is rarely prompt payment of royalties. Second, for the same reasons, the indigenous publisher is often unable to promote and sell the author's work both locally and internationally.[28] Thus, although the current regimes in Uganda, Rwanda, and Congo seem to be interested in promoting Kiswahili in their countries, Kiswahili publishers in Kenya and Tanzania have not seized the opportunity to promote their books in those countries.

The problems of publishing outlined above simply bring into focus the need for a coherent national book policy in both Kenya and Tanzania that would address squarely the problems faced by the publishers, including those listed above, and offer short-term and long-term solutions. It is by addressing the problems faced by publishers that the shortage of publishing outlets for Kiswahili writers can be solved.

READERSHIP AND DISTRIBUTION PROBLEMS

Most literate Kenyans, and all literate Tanzanians, can read Kiswahili. Hence, a potentially large readership for Kiswahili books does exist in Kenya and Tanzania. The problem of readership, therefore, has nothing to do with lack of potential readers; rather, it boils down to questions of relevance, accessibility, pricing (vis-à-vis the average income of the targeted audience), and book promotion and distribution generally.

The question of relevance in literature involves matters of content, form, utility, and interest level. This question can only be resolved by the author and his/her publisher. Generally, both good and bad books do exist in Kiswahili, and it is up to the reader to decide which books to buy and read. Note, however, that good literature need not be the most popular.

The problem of accessibility boils down to availability of infrastructure, such as public libraries and book distributors/sellers.

There are indications that Kiswahili speakers do read a lot. For instance, they are able to support more than 40 active Kiswahili newspapers and magazines. In Tanzania, data from the Tanzania Library Services indicates that many readers like to read stories, including translations from Russian and Chinese. Most Kiswahili books in the national library system are worn out, indicating that they are read frequently. One way of reaching out to readers would be to support the public library system by supplying it periodically with a given number of copies of each new creative literature title for distribution to its branches countrywide. The number of copies should be enough to enable the publisher to break even, and the author to at least recoup his/her writing costs. The figure of 2,000 copies per title has been suggested by Walter Bgoya.[29] In this way, publishers would be encouraged to publish more Kiswahili literature, and authors would be motivated to write more.

The public library systems in both Kenya and Tanzania need other forms of support, apart from book donations, to enable them to discharge their duties adequately and efficiently. Generally speaking, Kenya and Tanzania have an underdeveloped and dilapidated public library system, owing to poor financing by the government. The Kenya National Library Services (KNLS) was created soon after independence in 1963 to take over the public library services that were previously run by the EALB. Its other objective was promotion and establishment of public libraries throughout the country. To date, the KNLS has managed to establish only 16 public libraries and two reading centers. The majority of the 54 districts in Kenya are still without a public library.[30] The Nairobi City Council operates several libraries in the city, and there are a number of private, community, and institutional libraries. Nevertheless, the majority of Kenyans, especially in the rural areas, still have no access whatsoever to a public library.

The Tanzanian situation is no better. The Tanzania Library Services (TLS), established in 1964, is the national bibliography authority and the repository of legal deposit material. It inherited the library services and materials of EALB. TLS has 38 branches at the regional and district levels; it used to have about 500 village-level libraries, but these are no longer functioning. TLS runs a diploma-level school for librarians at Bagamoyo.

The initial idea behind TLS was to have a public library at every regional and district headquarters, but that could not be realized because of the economic collapse of the 1980s. Thus, four regions and most of the more than 100 districts do not yet have a public library today. TLS used to buy several hundred titles of each Kiswahili publication and distribute them to its branches, but now it no longer does that for lack of money. Indeed, for the last five years, TLS has been getting funds for salaries only. As a result, the library network and the bibliographical services have stagnated, numerous highly qualified workers have left the service, and its buildings are crumbling.

TLS stocks old, creative literature books published locally, but most of its holdings are donations from overseas. New local publications are no longer acquired, unless donated as legal deposit. Thus, a survey I carried out in 1996 indicated that TLS had only added five novels, five plays, and 10 poetry collections to its meager stock of local, mostly Kiswahili, Tanzanian creative literature in the previous five years.[31]

In spite of these problems, TLS libraries are still popular places for readers, especially school pupils. Recently, TLS imposed a small fee for library use, an unfortunate development reflecting the extreme penury faced by the library services. Nevertheless, that fee has only reduced, not stopped, the stream of young readers who flock to the library. Hopefully, that unfortunate charge will be removed when the financial situation improves.

The presence of bookshops and book distribution channels relies on the presence of a market. This relates to the existence of a book-buying public with the means to make purchases regularly. There is no question that a fairly big book-buying public for Kiswahili books exists today. Theoretically, about 50 percent of the 100 million Kiswahili speakers are literate. Assuming that only 10 percent of these people read books, we have a potential audience of five million readers. If we could succeed in encouraging each one of these people buy just one book per year, they would buy five million copies. At a print run of 5,000 copies per title, that would amount to 1,000 titles! Recent UNESCO statistics indicate that current production of all types of books in all languages in Kenya and Tanzania stands at about 600 titles per year.[32] With greater effort and a better distribution network, one should surely be able to sell more books!

The reasons why many books do not sell should be sought in lack of distribution channels, absence of bookshops, inadequate promotional efforts, incorrect pricing, and content and aesthetic problems, including low level of interest. The infrastructural problems can be tackled by creating adequate distribution channels and reviving the bookshops. The problem of content can only be addressed by the individual publisher and author. They have to study the needs of their target readership and try to cater to those needs. And the books must be written in such a way that they are pleasant and interesting to read.

Another way of reaching out to readers is to set up book readers' clubs.

Members of the clubs would contribute some money every year, and would in turn receive a selected number of titles. Since such books would be bought in bulk by the club, they would receive a discount; hence the club prices would be lower than the bookshop prices. The club could be run singly or jointly by publishers, booksellers, and book councils. The so-called problem of readership is, thus, largely infrastructural and, to a lesser extent, cultural. It can be reduced by dealing squarely with the problem of book promotion, distribution, and sales.

In Kenya, bookselling is fairly well developed. Currently there are more than 600 active bookshops. There are also many supermarkets, groceries, and roadside kiosks and pavement vendors that sell books. Unfortunately, the bookshops are concentrated in urban centers; many rural communities do not have access to bookshops. The other problem with Kenyan bookselling is lack of a national distribution organ with a reliable country-wide network. The major distributor, the Text Book Centre, seems to be satisfied with the volume of business within Nairobi and does not bother to open branches in other districts. There are several other distributors, but they are mostly small, often undercapitalized, and are incapable of meeting the needs of the whole country.[33] As a result, publishers have to do their own distribution, thereby pushing up their overhead. The situation is exacerbated by the poor communications infrastructure in the countryside, which further increases transportation costs, thus raising the price of books even higher for nonurban buyers.

In Tanzania, the situation is worse. Almost all studies of the publishing scene in Tanzania have considered marketing/distribution to be a weak—if not the weakest—link in the publishing chain. The PATA study on the "Textbook Distribution Project" succinctly puts the problem as follows:

> The main distribution outlet of general titles have been bookshops, but the number diminished with the confinement of school books to TES. Currently there are no distributors of books in Tanzania and publishers supply directly to booksellers and customers. In most cases publishers are reluctant to supply books to bookshops on credit because most of them have poor records of debt payment.
>
> Mail order is not usually preferred by publishers because postal rates are high and the postal service is unreliable. Publishers complain that sometimes the cost of sending a copy by post is higher than the price of the book. Book selling and distribution in Tanzania remains [sic] the weakest link in the distribution chain.[34]

In order to understand how this weakness came about, we have to go back in history. Book distribution and selling in Tanzania began as part of the missionary drive "to spread the word of the Lord." Small bookshops were established in townships all over the country, charged with selling Christian publications of all sorts. All major denominations had their own bookselling networks. The Anglicans had the Dar es Salaam Bookshop (founded in 1929), with branches in nine towns, including Zanzibar. The Catholics had the Tanganyika Mission Press, based at Tabora, which served more than 30 bookshops all over the country. The Inland Church, based in Mwanza, had nine bookshops dotted around the Lake regions. The Lutheran Church had bookshops in various parts of the country. The Muslims also had their own book distribution channels, but they rarely engaged in secular bookselling. Only the traditionalists showed no zeal in promoting their beliefs through books.

Many of these religious booksellers also stocked and sold nonreligious books, especially textbooks and educational readers. Dar es Salaam Bookshop was, in fact, the main distributor of colonial school and general publications during the British period. In the 1970s, the Cathedral Bookshop in Dar es Salaam, a Catholic bookseller, was a major stocker of imported textbooks and general literature titles. There were also many nonreligious bookshops-*cum*-stationery shops in colonial times. Many more were started in the 1960s, including the huge parastatal, TES, founded in 1967. By the 1970s, there were about 120 bookshops all over the country.

A new government textbook production and distribution policy established in 1970 confined school book production and distribution to the parastatals, and set in motion the process of disintegration of bookselling in the country. Bookshops could no longer hope to sell textbooks, whose market was always assured. Hence, some began to close down or change their business lines. In 1982, the government declared that henceforth all textbooks were to be sold through TES. That decision proved to be the death knell of private bookshops all over the country. Even the Dar es Salaam Bookshop faced problems and had to close most of its branches in 1987. The Cathedral Bookshop in Dar es Salaam stopped selling secular books and concentrated on religious publications. The University of Dar es Salaam Bookshop began to stock religious and Soviet publications in greater numbers, having failed to secure foreign exchange to import academic books. Many other former big booksellers, such as the International Bookshop and Book Distributors Tanzania Ltd., withdrew quietly from the book business. In place of bookshops, the phenomenon of second-hand book vendors operating on the streets came to dominate the bookselling scene.

The situation today is quite miserable. Although Pearce lists about 125 bookshops in existence throughout the country,[35] only about 10 are believed to be actively selling secular books. The newly resurrected Booksellers Association has only about 23 members, and it estimates that there are only about 50 operating bookshops in the country at present.

The existing booksellers have their own problems, the major ones being lack of capital and a reliable market. Some propose that a revolving fund for booksellers be created so that booksellers can borrow money from the fund to replenish their book stocks. The current deconfinement policy, which will eventually allow schools and parents to buy textbooks directly from bookshops, will hopefully enable some of these bookshops to recover. Already, new bookshops are being set up in Dar es Salaam to take advantage of this new liberalized atmosphere.

Finally, Tanzania, like Kenya, has no reliable book distributor with nationwide operations. This is in spite of the existence of a white elephant known as the TES. This monopolistic parastatal—created by the government in 1967, primarily to coordinate book distribution and manufacture and distribute school materials, such as exercise books and stationery—is now in the process of being liquidated. Yet TES has in place a developed nationwide book distribution network reaching down to district level, with offices, bookshops and sales outlets, warehouses, and even vehicles for ferrying books. TES still has 19 branches in various parts of the country. Five former branches that were in Singida, Lindi, Masasi, Ifakara, and Zanzibar have been closed down for economic reasons. TES still has warehouses in Arusha, Mwanza, Songea, Dodoma, Morogoro, Mtwara, Bukoba, Kigoma, Mbeya, and Dar es Salaam, although some of the facilities are presently rented out to businessmen whose businesses have nothing to do with books or education. TES also has branches with rented storage in Tabora, Shinyanga, Musoma, Tanga, Sumbawanga, Moshi, and Iringa.[36] The sad situation is that Tanzania has failed to use this well-established infrastructure to distribute books and is now forced to do away with it!

The TES management thinks that it can handle the distribution of books to all parts of the country, but most publishers I have talked to feel otherwise. They claim that TES is too bureaucratic and unwieldy, being a government parastatal, and, like most parastatals, is not immune to corrupt practices. Moreover, TES still owes some of them millions of shillings for books supplied in the 1980s! TES does not deny the debts; it only says that the books were supplied to the MEC, which failed to pay for them. In fact, TES says it is owed 400 million shillings by the MEC.

Under these circumstances, privatization of the TES into a joint stock company, with a clear mandate to serve as a national book distributor, would be the best option for the Tanzanian book industry. The new company would inherit the extensive network of bookshops and warehouses that are still owned by TES. In order to ensure that the new TES management does not divert it from its mission, stakeholders in the book sector, especially publishers, should have majority shares, with the government retaining a minority interest, in the company.

In addition to the new TES, other book distribution enterprises should be encouraged. For instance, right now there is a Dutch-supported book distribution scheme known as Network for Technical Publications in Africa (TEPUSA), which was set up in 1996 to promote book distribution in Tanzania. So far, the project does not seem to have achieved much in terms of taking books to the people. Certainly, a more effective and more permanent strategy is urgently needed.

To tackle the problems of accessibility to Kiswahili books, emphasis should be placed on the development of public library networks, including the introduction of book purchase schemes for libraries; the encouragement of book buying and reading schemes, such as book clubs; the promotion and expansion of the book distribution infrastructure; and the establishment of national and East African book distribution companies.

COPYRIGHT PROBLEMS

Unlike musicians and fine artists, Kiswahili writers generally have not yet faced serious copyright infringement problems. Of course, there are isolated cases of unethical practices by a number of printers, who secretly reprint and sell popular titles without the publishers' and authors' knowledge. Cases of copyright infringement of Kiswahili titles by foreign publishers have also been reported. There is, for instance, the case of Adam Shafi Adam, whose novel *Kasri ya Mwinyi Fuad* was translated and published in France in 1986 without his permission. There are also cases of Tanzanian writers whose books were published in Kenya without their knowledge or permission. In addition, there have been copyright rows between multinational and local publishers regarding alleged infringement of the copyrights of the multinationals. There was, for instance, the case of Evans Brothers versus Heinemann Kenya Ltd. (later EAEP) in Kenya in the 1980s regarding the novel *Kisima cha Giningi* by the late M. S. Abdulla. Evans failed to reprint the novel for more than seven years, but when it was reprinted by Heinemann, apparently at the request of the author, Evans sued Heinemann for breach of copyright and won the case.[37] A similar case arose in Tanzania in the early 1990s between an indigenous publisher, Mkuki na Nyota, and Thomas Nelson and Sons of the United Kingdom. In that case, a number of titles by the late Shaaban Robert, regarded as Tanzania's national laureate, had been unavailable in Tanzania for many years, though some were in great demand as required books in the school system. According to Tanzania's copyright law, an author's work becomes public property 25 years after his/her demise. Mkuki na Nyota applied that law to reprint a number of Shaaban Robert's titles in 1991 and was sued by Thomas Nelson for breach of technical—as opposed to author's—copyright. Aside from such isolated cases, copyright infringement problems in East Africa are still minimal compared to other parts of the world.

The two cases cited above show that multinational publishers are mainly interested in the profits they can make from local titles, not in developing local literatures or promoting readership as such. If the economic situation does not allow them to reap profits, or to repatriate their local earnings—as in the case of Tanzania—they are likely to keep the local titles out of print.

The Tanzania Copyright Act of 1966 is already out of date. For instance, it does not take into account developments in electronic technology that have occurred since. The act is reportedly being revised. One hopes that the new copyright law will offer greater safeguards to writers and artists. The Kenyan Copyright Act, Chapter 130 of the Laws of Kenya, revised in 1989, is more up to date, though it too may need further updating.

As far as international copyright conventions are concerned, Kenya signed them a long time ago. Tanzania procrastinated for many years, arguing that international copyright conventions largely served the interests of the rich countries at the expense of the poor. In 1994, Tanzania changed its mind and quietly signed the Berne Convention. The signing of the conventions by Kenya and Tanzania cannot be said to be a disadvantage for them since the two countries never utilized their nonsignatory status to pirate foreign works for their people's benefit, as was done by the USA, China, Cuba, and the former Soviet Union. On the contrary, it might be an advantage in the sense that the works of Kenyan and Tanzanian writers and artists that are in demand outside the two countries are now protected.

CENSORSHIP

Almost all governments, especially African governments, practice some form of censorship of literature and art, and Kiswahili-speaking governments are no exception. In the early 1970s, the ruling party in Tanzania banned a number of Kiswahili and English language publications ostensibly because they were "obscene" or offensive to some segments of the public, most notably the clergy and some conservative, ignorant, or hypocritical politicians. Among the publications banned at the time were semimedical books, such as *Jando na Unyago* by S. J. Mamuya; popular sensational magazines, such as *Baraza*, then published in Nairobi, and *Drum*; and David Maillu's "pop" stories. Soon a number of famous African literature texts, such as Mongo Beti's *The Poor Christ of Bomba*, Ferdinand Oyono's *Houseboy*, and E. Kezilahabi's successful first novel, *Rosa Mistika*, were banned from the school lists, reportedly at the instigation of Roman Catholic church authorities. Thus, the marriage of church and state in pursuit of largely retrogressive ends was graphically consummated.

The banning of a popular magazine such as *Baraza* deprived the person in the street of an interesting, if lurid, reading matter, and must have contributed to the decline of reading habits in the 1980s, for not many people were interested in reading and rereading boring party and government handouts. Unfortunately the lesson was never learned. In June 1998, three more Kiswahili papers were banned by the Tanzanian government for allegedly publishing obscene and insulting cartoons. I can only think of two reasons for the papers' loss of favor with the authorities. The first reason is their regular and biting exposure of the hypocrisy and immorality of those in authority. The second is their popularity. For instance, one of the banned papers, *Kasheshe*, had more readers than any other paper in the country and its readership was still expanding. That may have tickled the totalitarian instincts of the ruling party, which once enjoyed near-total control of the mass media.

Aside from such erratic acts by government, censorship in Tanzania has always been at a low level; many works critical of the government and the ruling party were published, and there were heated debates in the media and in other public fora, in the 1970s. I am not aware of any writer who was imprisoned, tortured, or hanged because of his/her writings during the presidencies of Julius Nyerere or his successor, Ali Hassan Mwinyi.[38] Unfortunately, at present that spirit of tolerance seems to be changing with the changing political climate. The people wielding power appear to believe that multipartyism means that only registered political parties have a right to discuss politics; any other organ or person can do so at his/her own peril—except, of course, when making statements in support of the ruling party! Thus, in the last two years, there have been many cases of journalists being arrested or threatened. In Zanzibar, where opposition politics is more heated, even nonsensational mainland papers, which do not toe the ruling party line, such as *Majira*, have been banned. Apparently, those in authority believe that there can be democracy without freedom of expression.

In Kenya, censorship has been used more often, and more devastatingly, as a political tool. Arm twisting tactics are often employed to force the media to either keep quiet or toe the ruling party line, and a number of writers have been imprisoned—or, more commonly, "detained without trial"—both for their political views and activism, as well as for their artistic orientation and practice. The most famous cases are Abdilatif Abdalla, a leading Kiswahili poet, Ngugi wa Thiong'o, and Al-Amin Mazrui, a renowned Kiswahili poet and playwright. Such repression has forced many Kenyan writers to go into exile, thus depriving Kiswahili and Kenyan literature of their much needed on-the-spot contributions. In the case of Ngugi wa Thiong'o, a number of his works written in Gikuyu have been banned, and those written in English and Kiswahili have been withdrawn from the school lists.

In conclusion, we can say that state- and religious-inspired censorship is one of the greatest obstacles to the development and flowering of Kiswahili literature and publishing in East Africa at present. This is a practice against which writers, publishers, human rights activists, and all cultured people will have to wage a protracted struggle.

ORGANIZATION AND COORDINATION

Professional organizations in the book industry include associations of writers, publishers, librarians, booksellers, and printers. All these—except a printer's guild for Tanzania—do exist in Kenya and Tanzania, and have often played a decisive role in promoting the interests of the indigenous book industry. In this section, I am more concerned with two types of organization that involve the writer directly, namely writers' associations and national book councils.

Writers' associations exist in Kenya and Tanzania. Kenya has the Writers' Association of Kenya (WAK). Information on the history, activities, successes, and failures of WAK was not available to me. Another Kenyan association that caters to Kiswahili writers is the *Baraza la Kiswahili la Kenya* (BKK—"Kenya Kiswahili Council"), which is based on the Kiswahili speaking Kenya coast. The Council seems to be mainly interested in promoting the use of "authentic" Kenyan coastal Kiswahili, as opposed to standard Kiswahili, which they consider to be a European imposition. The BKK also fights for preservation of the traditional poetic conventions, and sometimes organizes poetry writing and recitation competitions. There are other organizations, such as the Kenya Kiswahili Association, that cater mainly to teachers of Kiswahili in primary and secondary schools.

Several writers' organizations exist in Tanzania. The oldest is *Usanifu wa Kiswahili na Ushairi Tanzania*, the nationwide Kiswahili poets' association created in the early 1960s. There is also *Umoja wa Waandishi wa Vitabu Tanzania* (UWAVITA), the creative writers' association established in 1978. UWAVITA has branches in several regions. There are also eight regional writers associations, established under the auspices of the CBP, that are associated with UWAVITA. There is even a translators' association. Hence, writers in Tanzania do have enough organization to cater to their needs. What they lack is adequate financial and logistical support to enable the organizations to function effectively.

The other players in the book industry—such as publishers, booksellers, illustrators, and librarians—also have or are in the process of forming their own organizations. Hence, at this micro-level, the coordination of the people involved with books seems to be satisfactory. What is still lacking in both countries is an overall national book coordinating organ. In Tanzania, the CBP has been serving as an unofficial coordinator of the book industry since 1991; but the CBP is only a project and will not exist indefinitely. Hence, a more permanent national coordinating organ is needed.

UNESCO recommends the creation of national book councils. Such councils would serve as coordinating organs for the industry on both policy and operational levels. In the past, the idea was for such an organ to be governmental; current thinking inclines toward a more independent non-government—although government-supported—organization answerable to the book industry community. Such a book council should have a small, inexpensive secretariat that is efficient and nonbureaucratic. Its functions would be to coordinate all the stakeholders in the industry; seek funding for the sector; promote literature, publishing, and the reading culture; organize workshops, courses, and book fairs; offer literary retreats and study tours; offer awards and prizes to distinguished actors in the sector; defend and speak for the sector nationally and internationally; and advise the government on book sector policies.

Right now, book sector stakeholders in Kenya and Tanzania are working toward establishing (or reestablishing) national book development councils. In 1988, a meeting of book industry representatives recommended reestablishment of the Kenya Book Development Council (KBDC). The KBDC was registered in 1982 but has not been active to date. Kenyan authorities are said to be sympathetic to the idea. However, there are misgivings that a parastatal book council may not be the right step at this point in time, as it is bound to be too bureaucratic and inefficient.[39]

In Tanzania, a UNESCO-sponsored seminar for the Tanzanian book sector held in Dar es Salaam from 8 to 12 June 1998 resolved to create a book council for Tanzania before the end of 1998. A coordinating committee was appointed to prepare the groundwork for the establishment of the council, and is currently (June 1998) working on the draft constitution for the council. The Tanzanian Book Development Council is expected to be an NGO rather than a parastatal.

Conclusion

This chapter has discussed the state of publishing in Kiswahili from the point of view of the writer. It has revealed that the situation of Kiswahili writers in Kenya and Tanzania today is still precarious. The writer, though indispensable in the publishing process, is still generally marginalized, despised, and swindled, and largely disregarded. This bad situation is made worse by the socio-economic context in which publishing takes place—a context replete with financial, infrastructural, cultural, and political obstacles apparently directed against the book. The chapter has further shown how some of these problems are being addressed in the two countries by the relevant sectoral players.

It is regrettable that publishing in Kenya and Tanzania emerged in a situation of colonial contempt and disregard for "native" writers and their rights. This in time developed into mutual suspicion, antagonism, and hence polarization of the author-publisher relationship. Unfortunately, the average postindependence publisher usually tended to perpetuate this anomalous tradition, thus making a bad situation worse.

Now, as we move into the twenty-first century, we need a new beginning, a "New Deal" as proposed by the 1998 Arusha 3 Seminar, which clearly and decisively addresses this anomaly and lays the groundwork for future ethical relations between publishers and authors. Writers and publishers in Tanzania already are working toward that end.

The other problems besetting the industry, such as lack of skills and motivation for authors, lack of publishing capital, distribution and marketing problems, and language issues can only be addressed within an informed and comprehensive national book policy that neither Kenya nor Tanzania has in place at present. Such a policy should, ideally, be drafted by book sector stakeholders, possibly through the book councils, if they have been established. The draft should then be submitted to the governments for approval and adoption. That way, the industry will ensure that all the pertinent issues are fully and concretely addressed.

That aside, publishing in Kiswahili, essentially a phenomenon of the twentieth century, will fare much better in the twenty-first century, in line with the unprecedented expansion and use of Kiswahili in more and larger areas within and outside East Africa. Current developments in Congo

(Zaire), Rwanda, and Uganda indicate that Kiswahili writers and publishers will have a busy time in the future, provided they seize the time and play their part aggressively, sensibly, and ethically.

Notes

1. Publishing in Kiswahili occurs mainly in Kenya and Tanzania. Kiswahili publishing in Uganda is negligible. In Congo (Zaire), Kiswahili publishing is mainly for religious and primary education purposes.

2. The necessity for a *lingua franca* is explained by the fact that there are more than 350 different languages in the region served by Kiswahili.

3. The earliest papers include *Msimulizi* (U.M.C.A., 1888); *Habari za Mwezi* (U.M.C.A., 1894); *Pwani na Bara* (Lutheran, 1910); and *Rafiki Yangu* (Catholic, 1910).

4. The IKR took over the research and publishing functions of the former East African Swahili Committee.

5. Ruth Makotsi and Lily Nyariki, *Publishing and Book Trade in Kenya* (Nairobi: EAEP, 1997): 147–150.

6. PATA, "Textbook Distribution Project Feasibility Study" (Dar es Salaam: Unpublished Report, n.d.): 7–8.

7. The parastatal publishers, TPH and EAPL, are currently in the process of privatization or liquidation, and are thus hardly publishing anything.

8. Lucia N. Omondi and Kembo Sure, "The Kenyan Language Policy: A Historical Review and Research Agenda," in Birgit Smieja, ed., *Proceedings of the LICCA Workshop in Dar es Salaam* (Duisburg: LICCAP, 1997): 97–118.

9. Walter Bgoya, "Publishing in Africa: Culture and Development," in James Gibbs and Jack Mapanje, *African Writers Handbook*, Vol. I (Draft prepared for Arusha 3 Seminar, 1997): 66.

10. See Kenya Ministry of Education, *Education Kenya: Information Handbook* (Nairobi: Jomo Kenyatta Foundation, 1987): 90–114.

11. M.M. Mulokozi, "The State of Creative Literature and Publishing in Tanzania and Proposal for a Literature Support Project" (HIVOS and UWAVITA, Unpublished Report, 1996): 34.

12. poetry is by far the most popular creative, written art form in Kiswahili; there are probably no less than 5,000 practicing poets in Kenya and Tanzania. On this, see M.M. Mulokozi and T.S.Y. Sengo, *History of Kiswahili Poetry A.D. 1000–2000* (Dar es Salaam: IKR, 1995).

13. In Tanzania alone, there are no less than 40 Kiswahili newspapers and magazines that regularly serialize short stories and novelettes.

14. Up to now this practice has not changed. As late as 1992, a UK-based publisher tried to commission me to write a literature guide for a secondary school Kiswahili set book, and offered to pay me a lump sum of £50 for the work. Of course, I rejected the offer, and the terms had to be renegotiated to allow for royalty payment.

15. Quoted in *Recollections of James Juma Mbotela*, Joseph E. Harris, ed. (Nairobi: EAPH, 1977): 89–90.

16. Harris, ibid.: ix–x.

17. Shaaban Robert, *Maisha Yangu na Baada ya Miaka Hamsini* (Dar es Salaam: Nelson, 1968): 78–82. The translation into English is my own.

18. The seminar was organized by African Books Collective, in collaboration with the Dag Hammarskjöld Foundation, to address common concerns of publishers and writers. It was held at Tarangire, Arusha (Tanzania) from 23 to 26 February 1998.

19. The Jomo Kenyatta Prize for literature established in 1972 was discontinued after about six years for lack of funds. While it lasted, at least one Kiswahili writer, Abdilatif Abdalla, won the prize in 1973 for his volume of prison poetry, *Sauti ya Dhiki* (OUP, 1973).

20. Given the nature of the politics of international prize-giving, it is unlikely that the Commonwealth Literature Prize and the Nobel Prize would be offered to authors writing in indigenous African languages in the foreseeable future.

21. PATA, "Textbook Distribution Project Feasibility Study," op cit.: 7–8.

22. M.M. Mulokozi, op cit. (1996): 34.

23. PATA, "Feasibility Study for Book Production and Distribution in Tanzania" (Dar es Salaam: Unpublished Report, 1992): iii

24. R.S. Mabala and M. Kasembe, "Children and the Book Hunger in Tanzania," in PATA *Third International Book Festival* bulletin (Dar es Salaam: PATA, 1991): 23.

25. D. Pearce, "A Plan for a Children's Book Project Tanzania" (Dar es Salaam: CODE, 1990).

26. Up to 60 percent of EAEP's income derives from Kiswahili titles (Henry Chakava, personal communication to the present writer during Arusha 2, March 25, 1996).

27. Sven Hamrell and Olle Norberg, "Loan Guarantee Programs for the Developing of Autonomous Publishing Capacity in Kenya," in *Publishing and Development in the Third World*, ed. Philip G. Altbach (London and Nairobi: Hans Zell Publishers and EAEP, 1992): 421–423.

28. The creation of the African Books Collective (ABC) in 1989 was an attempt by indigenous African publishers to address this problem.

29. Walter Bgoya, "The Challenge of Publishing in Tanzania," in *Publishing and Development in the Third World*, ed. Philip G. Altbach (1992): 181.

30. Ruth Makotsi and Lily Nyariki, *Publishing and Book Trade in Kenya* (Nairobi: EAEP, 1997): 54–55.

31. M.M. Mulokozi, op cit. (1996).

32. Cf. *UNESCO Statistical Yearbook* (Paris: UNESCO, 1993).

33. Makotsi and Nyariki (1997, see note 24 above) list nine distributors (p. 163).

34. PATA, op cit. (n.d.): 10–11.

35. D. Pearce, "A Plan for a Children's Book Project Tanzania" CODE, Dar es Salaam.

36. Cf. Hassan Kabali, "Distribution and Selling of Books in Tanzania," paper presented at the Round Table Discussion on Creative Writing and Publishing in Tanzania, Dar es Salaam, December 12, 1995 (Unpublished paper in the possession of the author).

37. H. Chakava, "Books and Reading in Kenya," in *Studies on Books and Reading* (Paris: UNESCO, 1983).

38. The case of the Kiswahili novelist from Zanzibar, Adam Shafi Adam, detained in 1971 following the assassination of the Zanzibar first president, Abedi Amani Karume, does not fit here because Adam Shafi was arbitrarily detained for purely political reasons before he became an established creative writer.

39. Cf. Henry Chakava, "Book Marketing and Distribution: The Achilles Heel of African Publishing," in *Development Dialogue* Pre-Publication Issue (Uppsala: Dag Hammarskjöld Foundation, 1998): 61; and Gacheche Waruingi, "Towards a National Book Policy for Kenya," in *National Book Policies for Africa: The Key to Long-Term Development: Proceedings of the ZIBF Indaba, 26–27 July 1996* Murray McCartney, ed., (Harare: ZIBF Trust, 1996): 54–55.

Acronyms used in this chapter

ABC	African Books Collective
BKK	Baraza la Kiswahili la Kenya
CBP	Children's Book Project for Tanzania
CODE	Canadian Organization for Development through Education
DHF	Dag Hammarskjöld Foundation
EAC	East African Community
EAEP	East African Educational Publishers
EALB	East African Literature Bureau
EAPH	East African Publishing House
EAPL	Eastern Africa Publications Ltd.
HIVOS	Humanistisch Institut Voor Ontowikkelings-Samenwerking (Netherlands)
JKF	Jomo Kenyatta Foundation
KANU	Kenya African National Union
KBDS	Kenya Book Development Council
KIE	Kenya Institute of Education
KLB	Kenya Literature Bureau
KNLS	Kenya National Library Services
KSES	Kenya School Equipment Scheme
MEC	Ministry of Education and Culture
NGO	Non-Governmental Organization
OUP	Oxford University Press
PATA	Publishers Association of Tanzania
TEPUSA	Network for Technical Publications in Africa
TES	Tanzania Elimu Supplies
TLS	Tanzania Library Services
TPH	Tanzania Publishing House
UNESCO	United Nations Educational, Scientific, and Cultural Organization
UWAVITA	Umoja wa Waandishi wa Vitabu Tanzania
WAK	Writers Association of Kenya

3

Publishing in Southern African Languages: History, Challenges, and Opportunities

Dumisani K. Ntshangase

Introduction

The term "African languages" is a rather loose descriptive phrase for a mixture of languages that are either mutually intelligible or unintelligible. For convenience, I will refer to southern African countries as those countries represented in the Southern African Development Community (SADC). The number of languages in the region can be estimated at around 328. These include dialects and substraits of languages under particular groupings. "African languages" will be used to refer to those languages spoken by the various indigenous people of the region. While Afrikaans—with roots in Dutch—should be called an African language, it will be excluded in this discussion for analytical reasons. For the purpose of this chapter, I will deliberately exclude English, French, German, and Portuguese, even though there are interesting regional variations of these languages.

This region also has had four different strong colonial masters. While the British colonized most parts of southern Africa—South Africa, Zimbabwe, Lesotho, Swaziland, Botswana, Malawi, Zambia, and Tanzania—the Portuguese held control over Mozambique and Angola; and the Belgians controlled Zaire. Namibia experienced both German and South African rule. These colonial masters had different language policies with regards to their colonized subjects. In Namibia, German and later Afrikaans were the dominant official languages. Even though the local languages were not suppressed, they were not encouraged to thrive. The British colonies, in line with the policies of "indirect rule," were encouraged to recognize and develop local languages while maintaining the dominance of English.

The Portuguese, the Belgians, and the French, on the other hand, had assimilationist policies. They believed that part of the total control of the mind, body, and soul of the colonized subjects was to convert them to *petit* members of the empire whose language could only be the language of the master. These different strategies of control had a direct bearing on the development of African languages in the region and, subsequently, the codification of and publishing in these languages. It should be noted that never before has an analysis of the language situation across the region of southern Africa been undertaken.

This chapter, in its quest for a regional approach, hopes to open discussion on language issues from a nonpolitical boundary perspective. It is essential, if the ideals of economic and cultural development in southern Africa are to be realized, that we begin to talk of regional development. International experience has shown that regional development is essential for the development of member states. This also includes the role of language management and development. A regional approach to language issues is far more important than localized efforts.

Christianity and Early Writings in African Languages

It is now common knowledge that the modern forms of writing in African languages began with the advent of Christianity—even though there were earlier symbolic expressions of writing, such as the Khoi rock paintings, pottery and beadwork design, and hut decorations. The British missionaries mainly realized that the best way to convert Africans was to use their languages in the process of conversion. Thus, they not only learned languages where they were stationed, but also attempted to understand the ethnography of the colonized. To have converts and would-be converts understand and believe their message, and also to dissuade them from traditional practices that were seen as directly contradictory to Christian practices, missionaries had to use the local languages.

The translation of the Bible into African languages was the first exercise to put these languages into written form. Christianity is a religion based on a fundamental text. It was essential for converts to read the Bible and communicate the text in local languages. The priority was to render the text into the local languages and then use this as a basis for teaching. Once the foundations of the systems had been set, missionaries then used local converts to assist them in the spread of Christianity. Thus, basic literacy—reading, writing, and numeracy—and the formal creation of the *school* were means not only for spreading Christianity but also for sustaining it. It was from mission converts that translations of other Christian-related materials ensued.

Translations after the Bible included hymns, songs, catechisms, and other genres directly translated from English. Africans also composed their own versions that maintained the spread of Christianity and its sustenance among the converts. French and Portuguese missionaries, on the other hand, insisted on using the language of the colonizer as the language of conversion. While they were able to study the local languages and gain some understanding of the ethnography of the colonized, they maintained the dominance of French and Portuguese. Very little attempt was made by these missionaries to produce translations of the Bible and other Christian texts in local languages; nor did they encourage the use of local languages as a basis for the spread of their work. However, they encouraged the development of schools and it was in the school that a divide between the converts and the nonconverts became visible. The converts could speak the language of the missionaries and the nonconverts could not.[1] The development of the *school*—defined here as a system rather than only as an institution—enabled missionaries to create a sustainable environment for their work. However, this often tore communities apart by creating two factions within local communities—the converts and the nonconverts.[2]

There is very little deviation in practice between Portuguese and French mission converts; however, there are distinct localized forms of Christianity among converts from English missions. The expansion of independent churches that used African languages and derived practices from African tradition beginning in the late nineteenth century was more prevalent in English mission converts than their French and Portuguese counterparts. Thus, the process of assimilation among the French and the Portuguese was not only a direct result of the politics of the colonial masters but also of the works of the missions, as was the encouragement of African languages, rather than African culture, in English-based missions.

Toward the end of the nineteenth century, it was not only overtly Christian works that were being translated into African languages but general books and texts that lent themselves to Christian morality. The translation of Bunyan's *Pilgrim's Progress*, for example, was another means to perpetuate Christian morality. There were other forms, such as stories, travel, and adventure anecdotes by missionaries and European traders. There were lexicographical works done in African languages, such as the *English-Kafir Dictionary* in the 1880s. African languages and African ethnography lent much to the study of humanities in later years. By the turn of the twentieth century, Christianity had become a self-sustaining institution in Africa.

Converts and the schooled were now undertaking missionary work with more success than the direct intervention of the missionaries. It should not be misconstrued that Africans were passive agents in their conversion.

Some actively partook in the assistance of missionary activities and had independent motives and aspirations. The first educated Africans, such as Tiyo Soga, were able to present mission work with much desired public legitimacy. This was used as a sign that through education Africans could transcend into better beings, a theme that was also forwarded by educated converts even up to the 1930s. In fact, it was Tiyo Soga who translated Bunyan's *Pilgrim's Progress* into Xhosa.

At the same time, there were very few mission stations in Namibia. It should be noted that mission interest in the various regions of southern Africa was not centrally coordinated, even though there were structures, such as the British and Foreign Bible Society, that combined all, if not most, of the missionaries in the region. The language and political differences among the missionaries themselves are not the focus of this discussion but they cannot be seen as a monolith. There were other Africans, like Soga, who went on to represent the aspirations of the missionaries and also saw themselves as global citizens. Such practices continued well into the 1950s; most of the political leadership of African communities was drawn from this class.

The influence of Christianity continues even today. Most books written in African languages reflect a very strong Christian flavor. These can be seen in all forms of writing, including children's books, literature, and grammar books. While there are other forms of religion in the region, it still remains largely a Christian-dominated area. Although there are laws in South Africa that promote and protect the development and existence of other religions, the same cannot be said of other countries in the region. With the exception of "African culture" of the type that can be and is used as a means of political control—exemplified by former Zairian dictator in Mobuto Sese Seko's style of leadership—no other Southern African country promotes pluralism.

1910–40: A New Wave in Original Works by Africans

By 1910, there were very few books in African languages other than those with direct association to Christianity. However, a widening interest in the use of African languages was emerging. *Imvo Zabantsundu* (Xhosa), *Ilanga lase Natali* (Zulu), *Umteteli wa Bantu* (Xhosa), *Koranta ea Becoana* and *Tsala oa Becoane* (Tswana) were popular newspapers that either were written exclusively in an African language or had a balanced mix of an African language and English. Although some of these newspapers date back to the last few years of the nineteenth century, their mass appeal was only to be realized after the 1910s. In the case of *Ilanga*, its distribution reached even the Shona and Ndebele in Zimbabwe (then Rhodesia), as well as gold-mining migrant communities in Mozambique and Malawi. It was these newspapers, and to a lesser extent the *Bantu World*, that popularized the use of African languages as media for mass communication.

These newspapers also regularly published poems, short stories, and folktales in African languages, in addition to letters debating the state of African languages. It is of interest to note that no African language newspaper existed outside the physical borders of South Africa. None of these newspapers in African languages exist today, with the exception of *Ilanga*, which is predominantly read by the Zulu-speaking people—who are found in Zimbabwe, as well. Today, there are magazines in African languages, such as *Bona*, that have a competitive circulation, a niche monopoly, and a loyal market. With the exception of Kiswahili, to which a chapter is dedicated in this book (chapter 2), none of the languages in southern Africa had been used as popular languages for books outside South Africa.

While there still were no creative works of note in African languages by 1918, there were plans afoot to start what was to become the single-most important institution responsible for the development of African languages in southern Africa. Clement Martyn Doke can be regarded as the father of African languages in southern Africa. His work on African languages across South Africa, Botswana, Zimbabwe, Malawi, and Zambia established the creation of a credible study of African languages and inspired the publishing of books in these languages. When the Department of Bantu Studies—now African Languages and Literature—was established at the University of Witwatersrand in 1922, virtually no single study was available in and/or on African languages other than missionary works and travel and adventurer's anecdotes.

It was through the effort of Doke that African languages begun to be studied and developed comprehensively in southern Africa. Doke also made enormous contributions to the translation of Christian materials into other languages in Zimbabwe and Zambia. Though an academician and a researcher, Doke, armed with a Bible and a pen, was a missionary in the true tradition of missionaries before him. Doke's interest in Nguni languages and ethnography offered scholars direction and a base for further research and development. By 1933, Doke had managed to collect sufficient data for his study on Zulu, Sesotho, and Shona. He had also managed to create an interest in setting up a publishing list for books in African languages that later became the *Bantu Treasury List* under the Witwatersrand University Press. Doke stands as a tower of knowledge and inspiration to students of African languages south of the Sahara.

The Bantu Treasury is the only publishing house south of the Sahara that published books in Zulu (B.W. Vilakazi, N.N.T. Ndebele, and E.

Zondi), Sesotho (Mofokeng and Mocoancoeng), Tswana (Sol Plaatje and Raditladi), Xhosa (Mqhayi and Jolobe), and Kiswahili (Hitchens and Shabaan Robert) before 1940. Although the Bantu Treasury List was unable to sustain its growth after Doke left, it still remains the single most impressive list in African languages before the 1950s.

No publisher in the region has been able to match or generate the quality of those works, most of which still remain classics or are highly used in African languages today.[3] This does not mean that books published in African languages over the decades have been of poor quality compared to those in the Treasury List; rather, there has not yet been an elaborate and conscious branding of books in African languages comparable to that of the Witwatersrand University Press. While the press can boast of such a list, it also has not been able to produce even a single book in an African language since then.

Witwatersrand University Press was not the only press publishing books in African languages at the time. There were mainly missionary presses, such as Lovedale, that published works in African languages. In fact, the first African language book was published in 1919 and could be the first work of fiction by an African in an African language in southern Africa. By the end of the 1920s, there were prominent writers in African languages, such as the playwrights and satirists, R.R.R. Dhlomo and H.I.E. Dhlomo, who were brothers, the politician Solomon Tshekisho Plaatje, the Malawian-born trade unionist Clemens Kadalie, and many others who had published their works in newspapers. However, in scale and contribution, the Witwatersrand University Press was the key publisher responsible for the output of creative works in African languages.

Missionaries had established publishing presses within their missions. Those of note in South Africa were Marianhill, Lovedale, Tigerkloof and Morija in Lesotho (mainly for Sesotho), Vuga Mission Press, and Ndanda Mission Press. Many others operated in Tanzania. It was these presses, a continuation of the work of missionaries, that provided an opportunity for writing and publishing in African languages. B.W. Vilakazi's book *Noma Nini*, later published by Marianhill, was the first popular work in an African language. Having been submitted as a manuscript in 1932 to a literary competition at the University of London's School of Oriental and African Studies (SOAS), it was only published as a result of its potential for massive appeal.

Thomas Mofolo wrote *Chaka*, a classic in Sesotho literature that was later translated into many African and European languages. He started his manuscript in 1905 and completed it in 1909. It was finally published in 1925 by Morija Press. This was after much persuasion by the publisher for Mofolo to change his manuscript because it feared that the book glorified the Zulu king, something that was considered to be contradictory to the values promoted by missionaries and colonialists.[4]

By the 1920s, perhaps the single-most important advocate for the development of African languages and its literature was Sol Plaatje. By 1923, Plaatje had translated Shakespeare's *Comedy of Errors, Julius Caesar,* and *Much Ado About Nothing,* but had been unable to publish any of these. His translation of *Comedy of Errors,* as *Diphosho-phosho* (a literal translation of Mistakes-by-Mistakes), was finally published in 1929 by Morija Press, whose main activity was with Sesotho rather than the London Missionary Society's institution based at Tigerkloof. It was Plaatje, who was publicly known for his criticism of the missionary structures, that had taken charge of the orthographies not only of Tswana but of other languages. Plaatje had a keen interest in Tswana folklore and had collected numerous proverbs and folktales that later culminated in a manuscript entitled "Traditional Native Folktales and Other Useful Knowledge."[5]

When B.W. Vilakazi was appointed language assistant in the Department of Bantu Studies in 1933, he became the first African staff member to teach at a white university. At that time, the University College of Fort Hare, the only residential tertiary institution for Africans in southern Africa, had not made any headlines in its pursuit of African language promotion. It was Doke and Vilakazi of the University of Witwatersrand and G.P. Lestrade of the University of Pretoria who became synonymous with the intellectual study of African languages. It was from the three of them that publishing in African languages could actually be traced.[6]

Between 1904 and 1932, various presses published primary readers (or primers) in African languages. However, it was only in 1928 that a careful approach to the development of readers in African languages was developed. When Vilakazi joined the university, both Doke and Lestrade were able to access various languages with a degree of success. By 1935, readers in African languages, mainly translations from British primary readers, and European folktales were used for basic literacy programs. In addition, original works were created or commissioned and usually edited, rewritten, or consulted by Doke, Lestrade, and Vilakazi. This was the beginning of a boom in basic primary education among Africans.

The 1930s could actually be described as the real beginning of serious writing, rather than publishing, in African languages. In contrast to popular music, books were few and far between, but writers were able to attract the public's attention, primarily in urban African centers. Zulu, Sotho, Xhosa, Tswana, and Shona were increasingly visible. Tsonga, or Shangaan— spoken in both South Africa and Mozambique though it had a visible migrant community in and around the mining centers—and Pedi, spoken by the second-largest migrant community in and around the mines, were not yet languages of the school or of book publishing. The 1930s were the only period that enabled African artistic creativity to transcend to the popular before the 1950s. In addition to music, a growing reading and poetry culture was evident in the 1930s. No other period has since been able to generate as much public debate on the role and status of African languages and the books published than this period.

Whether this was due to the sudden collapse in the popularity of the Industrial Commercial Union (ICU), led by the charismatic Clement Kadalie, economic depression, or a remarkable growth in urbanization remains to be studied. What is evident from letters to editors of newspapers is that there was an urban cultural boom by the 1930s that cut across the borders of southern Africa. Coincidentally, it was in this period that segregation became firmly articulated as an official ideology, and it was in this period that the African intelligentsia developed its own ideology and voice.

1950–57: A Turning Point?

In southern Africa, commercial publishers, such as Juta, Perskor, Maskew Miller, Shuter & Shooter, Longmans, and many other small indigenous publishers, were involved in publishing various books. However, none of them had taken keen interest in African languages prior to the mid-1930s. In fact, very few of them had realized the potential of publishing in African languages. Other than English, which remained the interest of mainly (though not solely) the English publishers, Afrikaans was increasingly popular. Afrikaans, a hybrid of Dutch that had been appropriated as a nationalist symbol by descendants of Dutch settlers residing in South Africa, became the single most important publishing language. While this reflected white nationalist politics, it also symbolized the emergence of a fledgling Afrikaans middle class. By the turn of the 1950s, there were Afrikaans newspapers, magazines, and publishers such as Perskor.

There were various factors that mediated the growth of publishing in African languages in the 1950s. One followed the upsurge in Afrikaans publishing that was linked to the growth of Afrikaner nationalism and its institutionalization. This was the age of nationalism and the consolidation of African nationalism formed part of this new wave. In Mozambique and Angola, there was an intensification of the transition from protest politics to resistance politics that led to armed conflict in later years. In Britain, there was waning interest in sustaining influence in the region via its protectorates—Botswana, Lesotho, and Swaziland—in the face of growing local demand for self-governance and a return to monarchy. In South Africa, the National Party took power and was bent on making apartheid policy succeed. In Malawi and Zimbabwe, there was a growth in Pan-Africanist politics. In Namibia, resistance politics against the new colonial power, South Africa, intensified.

Massive migration from the countryside to cities such as Johannesburg (South Africa), Maputo (Mozambique), and Bulawayo (Zimbabwe) created a situation in which governance in those countries could no longer force people back to the countryside. The increase of Africans who were products of mission education in the 1930s and 1940s and were trained as teachers afforded these governments with a reasonable pool of African teachers. For the first time in the region, we see state-initiated programs to deal with the "African question" in the cities, as providing education became a program of social control. There was then massive education provision between the 1950s and 1970s—the years just before the independence of a number of countries in the region. The countryside, though marginal compared to the city, reaped some rewards as well. In countries such as Zimbabwe, Angola, and Mozambique, farm schools, rural schools, and education and literacy programs were introduced by governments concerned that the countryside, unless properly controlled, could offer launching zones for armed resistance against the colonizers.[7]

In this quest to provide mass education to Africans, the role of African languages could not be ignored. We can safely say that the 1950s provided a series of discussions on the role of African languages and language-management systems in the region. With the exception of Mozambique and Angola, where Portuguese was the only language of education and government, African languages were seen to have a role to play in the region. It was recognized that the best way to provide education to Africans was through African languages, but in ways where the dominance of English—and Afrikaans in South Africa—would not be undermined. The reasons for affording African languages a space in the education system were not philanthropic, but for the political benefit of the ruling class. The irony of this is that, just like apartheid homeland policies, it created favorable conditions for the development of African languages.

In South Africa, this was exacerbated by the apartheid policy that ultimately led to the creation of homelands. With all of these factors, it became abundantly clear that African languages would play a vital role in the history of the country. There were many books in African languages published in this period. These books were not only published by university and missionary presses, but also by commercial publishing companies. During this period, however, the government was neither in a position nor willing to provide massive funding for book provision in African education; demand for education, though, ensured a market. The number of books in African languages, primarily languages spoken in South Africa, Botswana, Lesotho, Swaziland, and Zimbabwe, multiplied in this period. They included primary readers, literature such as novels, poetry, drama, and folklore, and topical books on gardening, manual labor, and similar subjects directed at providing pre-labor education. With the exception of Namibia, there were similar plans in the entire region. In addition to this, there was a massive increase in African language studies. Eventually, the triumvirate initiative of Doke-Vilakazi-Lestrade was superseded by other people who followed in their footsteps. Dictionaries, word lists and similar lexicographical works, and grammar books were published in Zulu, Xhosa, Sotho, Tswana, and Shona.

Other languages were given attention as well. Doke had managed to elevate Shona in Zimbabwe, but discussions about other languages in the region, like Tsonga and Venda, were just beginning. Soon studies of these languages and ethnographies of their speakers emerged. This became a starting point for the growth of languages used to educate Africans. There were engaging discussions on Isindebele in Zimbabwe and South Africa, and Chichewa and other languages in Malawi and Zambia. It was in this period, as well, that the consolidation of *Fanagalo*—a hybrid of various African languages developed in the mines and sometimes spelled *Fanakalo*—was seen.[8] Books, instruction manuals, and the use of this language as a prerequisite for working in the mines date to this period.

The boom in gold mining also promoted major interest in the sociology of the region. This business sector attracted laborers from the rest of the region and enabled the growth of urban settlements, primarily around Johannesburg. This period also saw growth in other sectors, such as manufacturing and the secondary and tertiary industries, as well as growing interest in the regional economy, where overseas and South African businesses were becoming established. These developments spurred more interest in the education and development of the African labor force. A direct beneficiary was African languages.

Whereas this period enabled the massive increase in the use of African languages at schools and the publishing of books in African languages, there was a general decline in the amount of reading materials in African languages outside the school and education system. Eventually, reading books in African languages for general interest and pleasure, the debates on African languages, the circulation of newspapers in African languages, and people's general interest in African languages waned. In hindsight, this era could actually be marked as the beginning of the period that characterizes the state of African languages today.

1970–1990s: Opportunities Abound

Publishing in African languages in southern Africa is very strong today. This is particularly so in South Africa. We can safely say that there are more books in southern African languages in the region than there are in the rest of the continent. Southern Africa is at the center of African language development and publishing. In order to put this into proper perspective, it is important that we understand the dialectical relationship between the development of African languages, on the one hand, and the development of a publishing industry, on the other. With the exception of the South African publishing industry, the profile of publishing activities in other parts of southern Africa is not yet clearly directed toward exploring available markets and potential areas of growth. Considering events from the 1970s until now, it becomes clear that there will not be a vibrant publishing in African languages unless there is state initiative on language developments.

Following independence, the Lusophone countries in southern Africa—Mozambique and Angola—adopted Portuguese as their official language. It then became evident that there were no programs developed in either country to cater to African languages. The absence of instruction in African languages at schools and the lack of strategies to encourage their use led to a situation in which the need to develop reading and writing materials in those languages was undermined. Therefore, it should be no surprise that there are very few books in the local languages of Mozambique and Angola—and no newspapers, magazines, or mass-produced materials in African languages.

The kingdoms of Botswana, Lesotho, and Swaziland (BLS), though linguistically homogenous, retained English as the language of the state but Swati, Sesotho, and Setswana respectively as national languages. The languages spoken in these three countries were also spoken and used in South Africa, creating a sufficient market for publishing in these languages. With the exception of Sesotho, which has different orthographies in Lesotho and South Africa, books in the other languages could be used for both Swaziland and Botswana.

The 1970s was also a period in which there was a systematic attempt by states to homogenize and standardize African languages. Particularly in South Africa, Zimbabwe, and the BLS countries, systems and structures, such as language boards, were created to provide standard orthographies for African languages and coordinate their use in education, broadcasting, and print. This was the beginning of the liaison between the state as the provider and funder of education, the language boards as overseers of the use of African languages in print and education, and the publishers as providers of books. It was the language boards, or similar structures, that prescribed the books used in schools. This alliance has continued until the present and is solely responsible for the massification of books in African languages, though it has been marred by corruption when members of the boards acted on behalf of publishers and their own financial interests.

The use of African languages in schools provided another incentive for publishing in African languages. Throughout the region, with the exception of the Lusophone countries, African languages were used at schools from grade one until the last year preceding tertiary education. This was a result of the language-in-education policies in the region. It should not be read that there was the consequence of regional coordination, but it is striking that there were similar, though uncoordinated, patterns throughout the region.

The 1980s altered social and political engineering policies in the region. The emergence of modernist thinking led to the introduction of English, especially in the Lusophone countries. The use of English, its instruction at school, and the state-initiated programs for English acquisition created space for a language debate. The argument of its supporters is that English provides accessibility to the wider global economy. Whether the debate around English is justified or not is not an issue of contention. The 1980s saw an increase in materials published for English as a second language (ESL). Many NGOs specialized in that field. Publishers devoted time and invested capital in the development of ESL materials. Multinationals such as Macmillan, Heinemann, and Longmans imported ESL materials that were either used as is or adapted to the southern African context.

The result was decline of interest in the production and development of African languages materials. Toward the end of the 1980s, a revived interest in African languages emerged. This was sparked by the looming end of apartheid, the call for a renewal of the economies of southern African countries, the end of civil wars, and the general revival of interest in southern African affairs. African languages once more received attention. NGOs, that specialized in reading materials, such as READ, started developing materials in African languages. Publishers created special projects for African languages, including translations.

These developments sparked campaigns in other parts of the region for a reconsideration of African language policies. Over the next 10 years, state-initiated programs for African languages grew. In Mozambique, African languages have since been used in primary schooling in addition to Portuguese and English. As the years progress, African languages will be taught at secondary schools and hopefully studied at universities. In fact, the Eduardo Mondlane University plans to become the center of both language policy and language development in Mozambique. There are mutual discussions between the southern African countries on the role of African languages, which can be seen as a positive sign for the development of African languages.

After independence, we saw either a complete absence or a relative lack of publishing activities in southern Africa, with the exception of South Africa and Zimbabwe. State publishing arose out of a need and a political will. There was a need for mass education and the speedy provision of book supplies. There was also a political will to undo the legacies of colonialism. Coupled with a sense of political intervention and a mistrust of white-owned big businesses, these were both seen as legitimate mediating factors for state publishing. However, the lack of a book provision policy, crumbling economies, poor quality and distribution controls, and a general unawareness of the complexities of publishing led to the encouragement of private publishing initiatives in the 1980s. Whereas the state concentrated mainly on textbook provision—to a large extent successfully, considering the economies of those countries and the massive burden placed on the new countries after independence—provisions were made for nontextbook materials, though on a very limited scale.

NGOs (nongovernmental organizations) and GNGOs (government-nongovernmental organizations) played a key role in providing books and reading materials in these countries. This not only included formal education materials, but also a large number of materials for adult illiterates, youth education programs, farm education programs, and social relief. Indigenous publishers, though very small in size and scope, also played a significant role. Once the state realized its control over book provision—primarily of educational materials—the process of privatization began.

State publishing is not likely to dominate publishing in the region in the long-term. At present, Tanzanian private publishers have been allowed to produce school books, and local publishers have won tenders with a 15 percent advantage over the prices of outside competitors. Angola and Mozambique should open up for commercial publishing in the next few years, an action that in Angola will bring down the virtual monopoly of the National Book and Record Institute and the Angolan Writers Union, and in Mozambique the National Institute for the Book and Record (now almost nonfunctional), the Historical Archive, the Scholastic Publishing House, and the Association of Mozambican Writers.

Multinationals were very prominent in the "creation" of a textbook culture in southern Africa, as was the case throughout the continent. Most language programs in southern Africa were dominated by multinational publishing, with or without joint ventures with local publishers. It was also multinationals that centered their publishing profiles in language programs. The success of both Macmillan and Longmans can be linked directly to the success of their ESL programs. While they did not publish only ESL materials, the association between these companies with English and their international profile, expertise, and in some instances arrogance enabled them to launch other programs, such as social studies, life skills, and children's books.

Low levels of literacy are also important issues in the region. Campaigns to provide massive literacy programs were intensified in the 1980s and had reasonable success, judging by the growth of literacy programs and organizations. However, illiteracy is still one of the biggest problems facing the region today. Unless this is properly addressed, the provision of books to desirable levels cannot be realized. The provision of books in African languages is linked to the provision of literacy programs both at schools and beyond. There are attempts by the region's governments to provide structures for literacy in primary education and for adults and the work force. However, this goal is undermined by the lack of political stability and proper planning in the region.

South Africa is in a much better position than its neighbors and is likely to play a more active role in regional publishing in the next few years. Currently, it is the only country with vibrant and competitive commercial publishing and no state publishing at all. African languages have been at the center of language policy, though for differing ends. Book publishing in African languages has been very profitable for publishers. Books have been reasonably good in quality and have played a significant role in national literacy campaigns. A regional focus on language development is currently emerging such that book provision will cross borders. However, South African publishers are going to be the major beneficiaries of this process, and care should be taken that this not happen at the disadvantage or exclusion of local publishers. Partnerships across countries is essential, but so is local development.

Previously marginalized languages and communities, such as the Khoisan, will receive long overdue development programs. The Khoisan communities stretch from the Northern Cape Province in South Africa to Namibia, Angola, and Botswana. There has never been any strategy among these countries for developing the Khoisan communities or their languages. There have been studies on Khoisan languages and communities, but there has yet to be a comprehensive audit of Khoisan ethnolinguistics. Individual researchers from universities, such as Anthony Traill of the University of Witwatersrand, have undertaken linguistic research, but with no leanings toward language plans or policy. Nigel Crawhall of the San Institute of South Africa, as well as NGOs in South Africa, Botswana, Angola, and Namibia, have worked on the development of the Khoisan. However, without the direct intervention of SADC and individual governments, there cannot be any meaningful change.

Of all the countries in Africa, South Africa has the most advanced and competitive African language publishing industry. In addition to educational materials and literature, books and other written materials, including magazines and newspapers, are available in African languages. South Africa also has a relatively higher level of literacy and development than its neighbors. It has better distribution and printing infrastructures, numerous—though politically and socially uneven—library distribution channels, a functioning broadcasting industry, and many bookstores and book centers. The country also has a competitive and vibrant commercial publishing industry with comparatively less threat from state publishing. Publishing in African languages is well alive in South Africa, differentiating it from the rest of the region.

Book publishing is not the end of the book provision process. Literacy, libraries and their use, book stocking, book shops and centers, broadcasting and the media, schools and education, and other areas are pivotal to the meaningful existence of a publishing industry in any society. Publishing is not a cheap industry and returns from it are not easy to obtain. It is linked to the general state of the economy of the region. Coupled with civil wars, general poverty, and dwindling political responsibility in the region, there cannot be any guarantees for the industry. Fortunately, events over the last few years show signs of hope.

Publishing in southern Africa will ensure that publishing in African languages thrives. The revision of the language policies of the countries of the region, the identification of strategic development programs, and the encouraging state of politics in the region for investment all suggest that conditions are improving. SADC can be seen as a regional force for encouraging responsible governance and attracting investment in the region, whether regionally developed or international. Southern African publishers have also begun a series of trial operations across the region. The combination of multinational and South African publishers in partnership with local publishers in the region is likely to bear positive fruit in the next few years. African languages are going to be at the center of this development.

Globalization and the Twenty-First Century: A New Era

At present, publishing in African languages is dependent on schools. More than 80 percent of reading materials in African languages are textbooks and adolescent literature, children's books (mostly translated from English), lexicographical works, and government-initiated social programs, such as AIDS education. There is a healthy balance between state, private, and NGO sectors in the region that ensures the development of socially responsible publishing. There is also strong indigenous publishing activity, with the exception of Swaziland, which is essentially a Macmillan fiefdom.

New publishers, varying in size and experience, have mushroomed over the past few years and should continue to grow in numbers. While most specialize in niche markets, some have already started experimenting with books in African languages. While the expertise in African languages and publishing is generally limited in most countries, it is hoped that the pool of expertise will improve with the high probability of increased tertiary entries in the region over the next ten years. There are also training programs in publishing, such as the graduate program in publishing offered by the University of Witwatersrand, the first of its kind in the region.

Other sectors of the economy are potential growth areas. Tourism, wildlife, and the hospitality industries offer many opportunities for publishing in African languages. The market for booklets, travel guides, and general language courtesy books will benefit from development in these fields. Over the last few years, tourism and hospitality industries have become huge revenue earners for the region, opening more business opportunities for publishers that respond to the needs of these industries. Governments are preparing themselves for a new look and this will require huge and sustained training expenditures. African languages will play a significant role in training public administrators. This will also have a spinoff for other industries as customer service becomes essential to all businesses. Competence in an African language is very important to all businesses and governments in the region, and this provides business opportunities for publishers.

There is a strong call for partnerships between the state, the private sector and NGOs for the development of a trade market in African languages. Bilateral trade agreements between and among countries of the region and others, combined with strong calls within SADC meetings and the recent Non-Aligned Movement Summit held in South Africa, indicate that the success of any nation-state is dependent on three elements. These include, as noted by UN General Secretary Kofi Annan, cooperation between business and government, the opening up of local markets to international trade, and the maintenance of a human rights culture. The modern reality is that no single country can survive alone. In order to achieve this, communicating with the local population can only be effective if local languages are used. This creates huge opportunities for publishers with vision. With the changes in language management systems in the region, a very high opportunity for general reading in African languages exists. The regional market is slowly being condensed into one vibrant macro-market. This creates a strong call for competition that will increase the quality and diversification of products. Central to all of this is the role of African languages to both corporate positioning and publishing programs.

With proper planning, writing in African languages is bound to spread. The increase in literacy levels, the interest in African affairs, the changing complexion of African cultural politics, and the massive support of the African renaissance indicates that writing in African languages should increase and diversify. African renaissance provides businesses in the region with a branding that has cultural and economic links. Whether this is African middle-class political engineering or not is not the issue. What is certain, however, is that it provides a business opportunity that can be capitalized. What better way of selling this dream than publishing in African languages?

While it is true that the publishing infrastructure in most parts of the region is weak, a realization that governments alone cannot change societies could lead to acknowledgment of the role of the private sector and NGOs in promoting the most needed publishing infrastructure. In Zimbabwe, for example, small publishers and NGOs played a vital role in starting up the national publishing infrastructure. Hence, all that states need to do is create a climate for the private sector and NGOs to experiment with ideas. This will also enable them to identify small language groups—such as the Khoi and the San—as niche markets.

However, this should be done with cautious optimism. At present, and at least for the next five years, writing in African languages does not have the potential to diversify beyond the education market. The concentration instead will still be on school textbooks, limited kinds of literature, and state-initiated programs. Studies in African languages are showing trends of growth (overall enrollment in African languages at universities and colleges across the region is increasing) and this is likely to inject new life into the discipline. With new academics, it is hoped that African language use will be driven to newer heights.

One crucial aspect of any language development program is strong interest in translated works. As Henry Chakava rightly points out, "Who ever remembers that *War and Peace* and *Anna Karenina* were written in Russian?"[9] Translation provides the host language and its culture with a window into the cultures of others. It enriches the host languages and its art. Unfortunately, there is very little translation from either African languages into English or the other way around. With the exception of Chinua Achebe's *Things Fall Apart* and Thomas Mofolo's *Chaka*, very few books of note have been translated into African languages. Worse still is that almost no books are translated from one African language to another. Publishers cite a lack of interest and small print runs. But the future provides signs that there will be more translations into African languages. Most translations from English into African languages are children's books. However, translations of children's books from African languages to English are very few. The same is true for translations from one African language to another. Over the next 10 years, there will be a sufficient pool of children's books based on original African tales or adapted from existing tales and fiction. There are publishers, such as the author of this chapter, who are keen to translate English works into African languages and vice versa.

While this may sound like a glorified picture of the publishing industry and African languages in the region, there remain many issues to be resolved. For instance, there can never be a viable publishing industry without clear book policies. The region has not yet developed a book provision policy. It has also not shown signs of its distrust of private publishing.

In addition, a huge divide exists between policy, planning, and implementation. Unless these are resolved, the region is unlikely to realize its publishing potential. Governments of the region have not been able to meaningfully engage publishers and other organizations in the development of African languages. While there are moves to resolve this, the pace is so slow that it reflects a lack of commitment. Books are a luxury; where the choice remains between buying a book and a loaf of bread, the decision is obvious. However, no country can develop without a reading culture. Books are central in disseminating information, changing and shaping opinions, and developing the minds of an educated citizenry. If the governments of the region do not realize the importance of a publishing industry, then the development of the economy of the region is also a dream.

Primary to this is the role of African languages. History has shown that once the language imperatives of a society are ignored, all social development programs lack the value of ownership in those processes. Unless people identify with social change and development, there cannot be any progress. What better way to enable people to identify with programs than through their own languages? This ensures that the gap between the rich, the *neauvou riche*, the emerging political class, and the poor and forgotten is narrowed.

South Africa has eleven official languages—nine African languages, English, and Afrikaans. While South Africa should be applauded for having taken a bold step in implementing a language policy that includes all the major languages spoken in the country, such a move should transcend mere political symbolism. The region should take a closer look at language management systems. Unless African languages are affirmed in some manageable way, there will be no reliable activity in book provision in African languages. Part of the formation of a community for the region requires investigating regional areas of commonality and language. The use of African languages in countries such as Mozambique and Angola will create a climate for the growth of these languages and an emergence of new business avenues, such as advertising, marketing, and publishing.

Languages in the region must transcend political barriers. If the region is to further unshackle itself from colonialism, it needs to emphasize programs aimed at the development of African languages. The Sesotho language is a good example. At present, the language is spoken in both South Africa and Lesotho, with a total number of speakers estimated at 7 million. However, there are two different orthographies for the same language in these countries. For a more efficient system, officials should adopt one orthography to enable Sesotho speakers greater access to a wider pool of materials in Sesotho. South African publishers produce 92 percent of the Sesotho books, but such books cannot be used in both countries because of orthographic, rather than linguistic, differences.

Such uniformity will enable the development of Shangaan (Tsonga) in Mozambique, Zimbabwe, and South Africa, and Isindebele in Zimbabwe and South Africa. Shared information and systems will benefit speakers of Setswana in Botswana and South Africa. It is essential that the issue of African languages should be placed on the agenda of development policies for the region. Representation by language bodies such as the Pan-South African Language Board have begun yielding slow results. There exists the inevitable realization that there is no political gain in allowing the same languages to be diversified by orthographies or in not opening up markets to publishers within the region.

Regional cooperation will lead to literacy campaigns, library systems, book distribution structures, education policies that are jointly recognized, and a host of other spinoffs across the region. This should be seen in the context of regional economic development that will support small-to-medium-sized businesses—in publishing, bookselling and distribution, and paper and print production—and promote the culture of reading. Regional cooperation needs a strong emphasis on the opening up of markets and the creation of a healthy environment in which businesses can survive and thrive. The region has more to gain from an open market, and it is incumbent that education in all its forms constitute one of those key areas that permit private sector activity. Publishing is better poised for the open market era than any other industry.

It should be realized that, unlike the common belief in past decades, multilingualism is a resource rather than a liability. Whereas multilingualism was seen as hindering progress and good governance, diversity and plurality today are considered essential for the construction of a nation-state. In many countries of the region, the emphasis is now changing from the need to check diversity toward celebrating, promoting, and protecting it. The multitude of languages in the region should not be seen as a problem but as a challenge and an opportunity. They provide niche markets and avenues for new ventures. They provide an essential opportunity for small-to medium-scale publishing operations and joint ventures between publishers of different size and focus.

The infrastructure for African language publishing is already up and running; now sufficient competitiveness in the industry needs to be encouraged, and market differentiation revisited. It could thus be concluded that publishing in African languages is viable and that it will continue to flourish once the regional governments create an enabling environment.

Notes

1. For a more elaborate study on the missionary activities in southern Africa, see in particular, Jean and John Comaroff, *Of Revelation and Revolution: Christianity, Colonialism and Consciousness in South Africa* (Chicago: University of Chicago Press, 1991).

2. See N. Etherington, *Preachers, Peasants, and Politics in Southeast Africa* (London: Royal Historical Society, 1978).

3. See R.K. Herbert, *Not With One Mouth* (Johannesburg: Witwatersrand University Press, 1994). There are extensive archival materials on Doke and African languages at Witwatersrand.

4. See D.K. Punene, *Thomas M. Mofolo* (Johannesburg: Ravan Press, 1989); R.H.W. Shepherd, *Lovedale, South Africa: The Story of a Century, 1824–1955* (Alice, South Africa: Lovedale Press, 1971).

5. See B. Wallan, *Sol Plaatje: A Biography* (Johannesburg: Ravan Press,

1984); John Comaroff, *The Boer War Diary of Sol T. Plaatje* (Chicago: University of Chicago Press, 1989).

6. This author is undertaking research for a biography of B.W. Vilakazi.

7. There is a large body of literature on resistance politics, migration patterns, and other social and political transformations in southern Africa.

8. Fanagalo is a mine pidgin created as a result of contact among various races and ethnic groups, which became adopted as a prerequisite for working in the mines of southern Africa.

9. Henry Chakava, "Working with Ngugi," in *African Publishing Review* (July/August 1994).

4

African Publishing and National Languages: The West African Experience[1]

Mamadou Aliou Sow

Introduction

On the verge of the third millennium, and at a time when the world is characterized by rapid development of new technologies of information, Africa is still described as an "oral continent." Without being totally unfounded, this perception seems to disassociate the environment and the social evolution of Africa from the context of globalization.

We could not analyze the actual scope of African publishing in local languages without taking into account Africa's oral traditions, which remain essential components of everyday communication processes for a great many people, especially those living in rural areas. But, at the same time, we should look at the future of the continent—because it is undoubtedly going to go through significant transformations. These transformations include the spread of a written culture and the modern media.

This assertion was acknowledged during a 1995 Berlin meeting of experts on the promotion of a reading environment in national languages. The meeting recognized that in societies noted for oral communication, multilingualism, and the strong presence of a colonial language, education is characterized by an almost total lack of written culture in local languages. Nevertheless, it is believed essential to link oral practices with the written forms of communication and ensure the suitability of knowledge in order to enjoy the potential of transformation that lies in the integration of the two.

The development of a written culture in African languages is still hindered by African political leaders. Very few countries in the continent give "working language" status to the local languages spoken by the majority of their population. This restricts the scope and usage of these languages for teaching and scientific research. Due to their poor utilitarian value, therefore, the written resources have had a very limited influence.

Cultural development necessarily requires the promulgation of linguistic policies. These policies can integrate, in a complementary and positive way, the notion of multilingualism on the national level and the development and promotion of a local publishing industry. Such a process would not inevitably lead to the exclusion of foreign languages currently used, such as French, English, or Portuguese.

Publishing in African Languages

Despite a significant number of studies conducted over the last decades, only a few exist regarding the status of African publishing in national languages. Comparative regional statistics, especially between French-speaking and English-speaking countries, show that the latter are definitely more advanced in terms of publishing in African languages. Differences can be found within French-speaking countries, too, due to, among other things, different levels of political will. The general context of publishing in national languages is affected by problems that are more or less consistent throughout the continent. These include low literacy levels, limited numbers of publications, exclusive use of foreign languages in the schools, absence of appropriate distribution networks, poor quality of books in local languages, and limited readership.

Only state publishing and nongovernmental organizations (NGOs) in charge of illiteracy eradication are generally active in national language publishing. These institutions produce teaching materials of limited standard that are used for literacy training. A brief analysis reveals three main groups of obstacles to publication in national languages.

Constraints in Writing

In most countries, writers in local languages have very poor logistical support and little motivation. Those who succeed in writing in local languages thanks to the textbook market are usually unprepared for the task. A few training experiments have been conducted for textbook writers by the German assistance agencies (DSE-GTZ projects) in Madagascar, Nigeria, and Mali. These experiments helped to create local competencies that foster modern techniques of writing. The techniques acquired in this exercise were then reinvested for the development of national language writing.

Authors find it difficult to get recognition from the government due to a lack of national writers' organizations. In western French-speaking Africa, only Senegal has a national language writers' association that efficiently works to develop a popular literature. The plurality of alphabets used in the transcription of languages is also a major hindrance for the development of local languages. For example, three scripts are used in Guinea: harmonized Latin scripts in lower Guinea, the Adjami alphabet with Arab scripts in middle Guinea, and the N'ko alphabet in upper Guinea. Sometimes, two alphabets are used simultaneously in the same area.

CONSTRAINTS IN PUBLISHING

State publishing in local languages has always been active due largely to multiple literacy campaigns conducted by these countries since independence. However, the experience of the last 30 years has shown that state publishing lacks sustainability and a mechanism for cost recovery. On the other hand, private publishing in most African countries still does not appear interested in this business venture, even though experts forecast significant potential sales in local language markets. As far as local capacities are concerned, publishing in local languages encounters the same problems as publishing in foreign languages. These include poor financial resources among the publishing companies, high production costs, an absence of distribution networks, and the lack of a reading culture within the general public.

CONSTRAINTS IN DISTRIBUTION

One last element that cannot be neglected in local language publishing concerns distribution difficulties. In most countries, coverage usually dedicated to literary issues in the media—print media, TV, and radio—do not offer any space for materials published in local languages. This lack of interest is detrimental to the survival of publishing in these languages. It is even more detrimental when we recognize the influence of the media on the general public. Book distributors in general tend to be less interested in stocking works in local languages. As a matter of fact, it is almost impossible to find local language publications in big city bookstores. As a result, local language products receive little popular exposure.

To foster publishing in national languages, we need also to consider the role of private publishers in the production and the distribution of good quality books with contents adapted to readers' needs, and, above all else, offered at an affordable cost. This could be achieved through an active collaboration with the state's specialized structures, NGOs, and private publishers. Moreover, the postliteracy era has to be a constant concern because the illiteracy rate has a great tendency to increase from lack of reading materials and poor, or even absent, public reading networks. As a whole, African publishing in national languages appears to be constrained by numerous factors.

The Guinean Experience

Guinea is a typical multilingual nation. About 20 different languages are spoken throughout the territory. Among these, eight are spoken by the majority of Guineans as their first or second language. These languages are Pular, Maninka, Soso, Kissi, Kpèlè, Lomaghoi, Wamey, and Oneyan.

Guinea declared its independence in 1958. At independence, the country quickly realized that the education system left behind by the colonizer was incompatible with Guineau's aspirations. The country's new leaders hoped to achieve total independence in all facets of life—political, economic, and cultural. Given this, French was considered an extension of the colonial system.

This concern seems to justify the importance of making the decision to introduce national languages into formal and informal teaching environments in Guinea. This decision was all the more important given the conviction that teaching in the mother language helps children to perform better in school. That is why for a long time Guinea was considered a "pioneer state" in the use of national languages in schools.

In 1969, the government undertook important measures to reinforce the policy of using national languages. The measures included the use of eight national languages as teaching languages in elementary schools, the obligation to write all political and administrative documents in French and in the national language, and the establishment of literacy diplomas in national languages at all levels.

The decade 1968–78 marks the most decisive phase of the use of Guinean languages. This era was rich in events and inspired some interesting and critical research. In 1982, UNESCO recognized the efforts of the population to eliminate illiteracy with its Nadejda Kroupskaïa award.

But after the use of national languages as a teaching medium for 15 years, French still remains the official working language. What conclusion can be drawn from this? Although we have witnessed a genuine political will to encourage indigenous languages on the national cultural scene, their introduction in the educational system has had inadequate preliminary preparation, creating serious problems. These problems include the multiplicity of the languages to be studied (eight), insufficient preparation of teachers, lack of appropriate educational materials, the limited amount of scientific research conducted on the selected languages, and integration problems for graduating students. Moreover, the country was under a centralized economic system and participation by the private sector in the production of written materials was hindered, hampering the endogenous production of school textbooks in local languages.

Documents in Guinean languages, especially school textbooks, were distributed for free to the targeted populations—students and teachers, political leaders, literate adults, and executives. This practice of handing out everything for free, as well as the poor production quality and the overt politicization of contents, contributed substantially to the books' depreciation.

However, certain developments emerged from this experience:

- It proved to many skeptical minds that African languages could be used as a support for technical and scientific knowledge;
- A printing office dedicated only to education and culture was created. Unfortunately, this did not play its role satisfactorily due to poor financial support;
- A department of national languages in charge of the promotion and distribution of books and educational packages for teaching in local languages was created;
- An Academy of Languages was created and placed in charge of developing a translation method for scientific words in national languages and the standardization of their spelling;
- An important lexicon was created for scientific words in six national languages; and
- A great number of school books and other popular works were produced.

When the language policy was changed in 1984, Guinea's new authorities faced a quasi-total return to the old system. One of the first decisions taken was to stop teaching in national languages and instead reintroduce French at all educational levels. The decision to reintroduce French was far from unanimous among national language researchers and specialists. The government faced public opposition as a result of the unpopular experiment with French.

Nevertheless, while waiting for future legislation aimed at the return of local languages to the educational system, private publishers, such as Gandaal Publishers, invested in the publication of general literature books in Guinean languages.

Local Language Publishing in French-Speaking West Africa

If Guinea played a pioneering role in the use of national languages in school, we see that the other French-speaking countries followed a slower but more methodical process for introducing local languages in their educational systems. This process can be characterized as follows: the stronger the political will, the more significant were the effects on the growth and development of published materials in national languages.

In Senegal, the government has always showed a genuine political will to promote national languages, initiating a large number of national language literacy campaigns and experimental programs for basic education. This political will is exemplified by the creation of a ministry in charge of national languages and other specialized services.

The University of Dakar and the Fundamental Institute of Black Africa (FIBA) have conducted important linguistic research, paving the way for a modernization of Senegalese languages. Although the production capacity and the distribution of books in national languages is relatively poor, they both look more promising given the involvement of some private publishers who print books in national languages such as Wolof, Pular, and Sereer.

Institutions such as the Department of Literacy and Basic Education (DLBE), and NGOs such as ARED, annually produce dozens of books in national languages on subjects dealing with basic training (reading, writing, and numeracy), and popularizing agriculture, sanitation, and hygiene.

In Mauritania, publishing in national languages is in its infancy, except for publications in Arabic. A few institutions, such as the Institute of National Languages and some NGOs, are struggling to eliminate illiteracy in the "triangle"—Mali, Mauritania, and Senegal—by publishing materials of particular interest to the rural community in black African languages. Generally, these are basic training books for reading and writing in the Pular, Wolof, and Sooninke languages. An experiment is also being conducted in bilingual schools in which both black African languages and French are introduced as second languages.

Mali has dynamic national language activity, particularly in certain parts of the country. The conceptualization of the new basic school program relies on a convergent use of national languages and French in primary schools within a framework of functional bilingualism. On the other hand, the national program for the elimination of illiteracy has been reinforced over the years thanks to programs created by the Department for the Functional Elimination of Illiteracy and Applied Linguistics.

The principle of convergent methodology recommends teaching in the mother tongue before introducing French. Today, this principle has become a reality: in the renewal of Malian schools, local languages have reclaimed the place that should always have been theirs. Owing largely to this policy, the country is experiencing strong publishing activity in national languages, especially Bamananka, Fulfulde, Songhay, Dogon, and

Tamasheq. The Jamana Cultural Cooperative produces and distributes the majority of the books. Other small publishing businesses, especially Fayida and Duniya Publishers, are also producing very high-quality materials. The Canadian Organization for the Development of Education (CODE) is another institution that has significantly supported the production and distribution of published materials in Malian languages. For its part, the Malian government has created the institutional tools that could help the rapid emergence of a conducive environment for reading in national languages. This initiative is largely supported by external donor and financial institutions.

In Burkina Faso, government authorities have taken into account the fact that a strategic change is necessary for implementing basic education. This is apparent in the creation of a few educational structures, such as "satellite schools" and centers of nonformal basic education, in which teaching takes place in French and in national languages. In the last 15 years, thousands of adults have learned how to read and write in their mother language thanks to national programs for the elimination of illiteracy that have benefited from government support and foreign cooperation.

The National Institute for the Elimination of Illiteracy has printing facilities that produce thousands of books and other publications annually. It trains people from the rural areas through educational activities in 14 different languages. As far as printing is concerned, the Institute plays an important role. No other private structure can presently match its activities.

In Niger, the number of youth and adult literates who have not been provided with formal schooling has increased. This is due to the large number of programs created by numerous NGOs specializing in education, and especially by the Department for the Elimination of Illiteracy and Training of Adults (DAFA). These NGOs offer training in eight different languages: Arabic, Fulfulde, Gulmancema, Hausa, Kanuri, Tamajaq, Tubu, and Zarma. The National Institute of Documentation, Research, and Educational Action has also produced a series of elementary school textbooks in national languages in cooperation with GSE (a German institution) and with DAFA.

Generally speaking, it appears that the practice of publishing in national languages has had difficulties taking off in the French-speaking African territories. Governments, private publishers, NGOs, and sponsors have to consolidate their efforts to promote publishing.

Opportunities for Publishing in African Languages

Today, most people concerned with African publishing, and especially political authorities, are aware of the vital role played by education for development. They know that they have to promote national languages to foster education and training.

Although the obstacles mentioned earlier still remain, some opportunities are clearly appearing. The current socio-political environment in West Africa is more conducive to fostering the use and development of national languages. The process of democratization that gained momentum on the continent a couple of years ago will also undoubtedly help this evolution. And in general, more emphasis is now accorded to the provision of information and popular education, especially among vulnerable groups such as women and children.

It should be stressed that national languages can benefit from better linguistic treatments by specialists interested in scientific and technical use. Harmonized alphabets—with appropriate computer software—have appeared in a few languages, and thematic lexicons have been substantially improved as a result. On the other hand, technical constraints affecting the endogenous production of books have declined, thus enabling more local industries to emerge. This enables the growth of rural media both on a qualitative and quantitative level.

It is interesting to note the establishment of a new dynamic that promotes coproduction and copublishing projects in national languages among African publishers. In fact, publishing is one of the most important channels for integrating Africa. Publishing in transnational languages could effectively contribute to the abrogation of linguistic barriers created by the official use of foreign languages.

For example, publications produced in Pular could be read by millions of readers spread across a multilingual western African region of Francophone, Lusophone, and Anglophone composition. The same is true for Kiswahili, which is spoken in the Anglophone countries of Tanzania and Kenya and the Francophone Democratic Republic of Congo (Zaire). The existence of networks such as APNET (African Publishers' Network) and GRAPELA (Action Group for the Promotion of Publishing in African Languages) is another force that helps the development of a local publishing infrastructure on the continent. These networks boost cooperation between African publishers and promote the emergence of a conducive environment for national languages.

The Publisher's Mandate

African private publishers play a critical role in the improvement of the state of publishing in national languages. They should therefore be able to take over the means of production and distribution used in promoting these languages. Moreover, while trying to promote their own local languages, African private publishers should also be capable of broadening their publishing scope to reach wider linguistic regions based on the most widely spoken African languages, such as Pular, Mandingue, Hausa, and Kiswahili. This initiative could help make these products more accessible to a wider public at an affordable cost. This could only be realized, however, if governments recognize the importance of national languages and the role private publishers play in promoting them by providing favorable business opportunities in the textbook market.

This requires an end to the dominance of important printed products by government-owned publishers. The acquisition of book production inputs should also be facilitated by reducing custom duties on these products. Easy access to financial institutions and a favorable business environment should also be created for private publishers. Other provisions that would further support local initiatives include the presence of a clear policy on national languages, the promulgation of national book policies that would facilitate publishing in local languages, the creation of efficient mechanisms of book promotion and distribution, the strengthening of literary activities, and the reinforcement of public reading environments.

Conclusion

While trying to improve the reading and writing abilities of the majority of its citizens, each country should integrate linguistic policy and the effective use of national languages into mainstream national life, especially as it concerns education and administration. Maintaining and enriching national cultures should also not be separated from development plans; national languages can provide base to make this possible. There is no need to demonstrate that the most appropriate language of learning is the mother language. What is needed today is to undertake important educational system reforms that would promote national language use, at least during the first years of schooling. The emergence of a conducive reading environment can only exist with appropriate educational policies. And these policies should fulfill the aspirations of the population for a genuine decolonization of the linguistic and educational practices.

Publishing in African languages will advance only if these prerequisites are fulfilled and only if we stop considering national languages as rural dialects. The role of African intellectuals here is significant. They are needed to help construct a better world for rural and urban populations that is in harmony with the global community. That is why all partners should be involved in the expansion of publishing in national languages to promote a genuine democratization of access to science and modern technologies for everyone. Sponsors should particularly support private African publishers who are active in the business of publishing in local languages. The results of such a process will be all the more efficient if transnational languages are used for basic education, as well. This process not only benefits from an economy of scale, but also favors a genuine cultural and economic integration of the countries that share these languages.

Note
1. This chapter was originally prepared in French.

5

The Politics of Multilingual Education and Publishing in Ethiopia

Damtew Teferra

Introduction

The main purpose of this study is to analyze the significance of the policy of the new government in Ethiopia on education, language, and publishing. Ethiopia is currently undergoing wide-ranging social and political changes of tremendous proportion. Among these changes, the policy on vernacularization of primary education is one of the most prominent. This study focuses on the implementation of this policy in Ethiopian schools and its impact on education and textbook production. The discussion highlights the pros and cons of implementing the vernacularization policy within the context of education and publishing.

Two interests prompted me to undertake this study. The first was the controversy over the replacement of Amharic as a medium of instruction by numerous other vernacular languages. This exercise, boldly fostered by the government despite numerous critical voices, is new to Ethiopia. The study also reflects contemporary views on vernacular languages used as media of instruction by drawing from the experience of other countries that have undertaken similar exercises. The experience is then considered against the background of the Ethiopian context.

My second interest was to examine how the campaign of vernacularization influences the production, publishing, and distribution of textbooks and other instructional materials for these newly developing languages, each of which has no history of writing, as well as poor or nonexistent literature. The capacity, capability, shortcomings, and difficulties of the Ethiopian government's major publishing and printing power house, and its effort to cope with growing and diversifying regional and national needs, are also discussed.

The Language Scenario

THE FACTS IN PERSPECTIVE

The issue of language is a very controversial and complicated one that brings political, social, economic, and cultural forces into constant interplay. Language issues have been sensitive both in developing and developed countries. They are contentious issues in Canada, Belgium, and, to some extent, Britain and the United States. The complexity of language issues in numerous developing countries, and Africa in particular, is compounded by its diversity. For example, India, Papua New Guinea, Nigeria, Indonesia, and Tanzania have 1,022, 850, 350, 300, and 120 languages respectively.[1] A more recent report by Daswani, however, reduces the number of Indian languages to a "total of 211 languages and dialects."[2] Today, there are more than 5,000 languages spoken across the face of the earth, of which sub-Saharan Africa alone accounts for about 1,200.[3] A recent report by Wedekind reveals that Ethiopia alone has 99 distinct languages.[4]

As Mazrui and Mazrui succinctly put it:

> Africa's ethnic heterogeneity is reflected in language. Per capita there is a wider range of languages in Africa than in any other continent in the world. By a strange twist of destiny, there are also more French-speaking, English-speaking, Portuguese-speaking countries in Africa than anywhere else in the world. In terms of ethnic units which use African languages as mother tongues, Africa is a continental Tower of Babel in all its diversity.[5]

They go on to say that:

> It is generally acknowledged that the African continent constitutes the most complex multilingual area in the world. The complexity results from the high numbers of languages, the way they are distributed, the relatively low numbers of speakers per language, and intensive language contact in many areas of the continent resulting in widespread multilingualism.[6]

In most of the colonized countries of the Third World, the language of the colonizer has served not only as an official common national language, but also as a buffer zone between the often competing interests of various ethnic groups. The metropolitan languages—English, French, and Portuguese—became more entrenched as modern education expanded its scope on the continent.

Though the medium of instruction in colonial Africa was predominantly the language of the colonizers, some local languages were also used in formal education. In West Africa, for example, Christian missionaries hoped to spread their religion by teaching people to read the scriptures in their own tongues and to show, through the study and use of the African languages, that those who spoke African languages were not less than human. The first school in Senegal, opened in 1817, experimented with teaching in Wolof and French.[7] Unfortunately, the "attempt made in the early years to use Wolof as the medium of instruction was abandoned and thereafter French became the sole linguistic vehicle for instruction at all levels."[8]

In August 1831, the first lesson in Yoruba was given in Charlotte's Girls School in Freetown (Cameroon).[9] The missionary linguists' contribution to mother tongue education is impressive in two respects. First, a body of material and a ready orthography for many languages became available through their work. Second, through their schools, at least in the English-speaking colonies, the missionaries established the tradition of beginning education and literacy in the mother tongue, which was to persist in the educational policy of many African countries.[10] The practice of vernacular education varied within Anglophone, Francophone, and Lusophone Africa; generally, the laissez faire British policy, unlike the rest, gave more room for the missionaries to implement vernacular education.

Of the languages spoken in Africa, the last to be captured in writing were the Afro-ethnic tongues. Although Amharic has had its own alphabet for several centuries, it was not until after the inception of European colonialism that some of the other Afro-ethnic languages, which hitherto had been exclusively oral, were reduced to writing using the Roman script. In a sense, then, while European colonialism and its language policies often posed a serious threat to Afro-ethnic languages, it also accorded some of them a greater capacity for self-preservation through the introduction of the written word.[11]

EDUCATION IN A MOTHER TONGUE: HOW SIGNIFICANT IS IT?

The movement to educate children in their mother tongue gathered momentum after a UNESCO conference of experts in Paris in 1951. The conference concluded that the best medium of instruction for a child is her or his mother tongue. Psychologically, it is the system of meaningful signs that works automatically for expression and understanding. Sociologically, it is a means of identification among members of the community to which he or she belongs. Educationally, the child learns more quickly through the mother tongue than through an unfamiliar linguistic medium.[12] A number of studies have been undertaken since the Paris conference that concur with and legitimize its findings. According to Sharma:

> No foreign language can take the place of the mother tongue and no system of education can afford to disregard it without serious detriment to the mental development of the child. Thought and language go together as soul and body. One is dependent on the other for its existence. They grow and decay together. The child thinks and dreams in the language through which he acquires the earliest firsthand experiences of life. This naturally happens to be the mother tongue. And for this reason the mother tongue becomes the first condition of schooling for the intellectual development of the child.[13]

Resnick also argued that mother tongue education is important because it is one of the chief means of preserving the best of native customs, ideas, and ideals, thereby preserving something more important than all else—native self-respect. He contends that no greater injustice can be committed against a people than to deprive them of education in their own language.[14] Gandhi noted that the use of a foreign language as the medium of instruction creates insurmountable difficulties for students.[15] He argued that, as a result of such difficulties, it takes about twelve years to obtain the matriculation certificate; and, even then, the general knowledge acquired over this period is pitifully inadequate. He identified two major problems engendered by education in colonial languages. First, students develop the habit of learning whole passages of required textbooks by heart. Second, a foreign medium does not merely occupy time in the curriculum, but limits what can be learned, eventually undermining the education process.

Certain narratives, such as local folklore, folktales, poems, songs, and riddles, are so culturally intertwined that they do not readily succumb to translation. They are a reflection of the cultural, social, economic, and political realities that created the very language. The provision of primary schooling in local languages thus brings the curriculum closer to home. Students can focus on the message without grappling with "designated" or imposed languages of instruction.

Tagore aptly frames the lack of congruence between students and their books in colonial-language schooling as follows:

> The books he reads paint no vivid pictures of his home, extol no ideals of his society. His daily pursuits of life find no place in those pages, nor does he meet there anybody or anything he hap-

pily recognizes as his friends or relatives, his sky and earth, his mornings and evenings, his cornfields and rivers. Education and life can never become one in such circumstances and are bound to remain separated by a barrier.[16]

Moreover, the scanty educational research on vernacular languages in Africa has come to conclusions that favor mother tongue education. First, research has shown that mother tongue learners score consistently higher in reading, arithmetic, and social studies than those learning in English (and that there are better home-school relations among the mother tongue learners). Second, it has found that differences between pupils studying in their mother tongue and those learning in a foreign language would likely increase. Third, it has shown that the English vocabulary of foreign language learners leaving primary school at the age of 12 or higher is smaller than their vernacular vocabulary on arrival at 6 plus and also lower than the vocabulary of English children leaving an infant school. Fourth, it has found that there is a loss of learning through using English, or probably any other foreign language for that matter, as a medium of education. And fifth, it has shown that children are at their best when taught in their mother tongue and asked to recall lessons in the same language.[17] Although the results of different studies are surprisingly mixed, Woodhall concurs that many educators believe that teaching children in their mother tongue is more effective than teaching in a foreign or "imposed" language, particularly during the early years of primary education.[18]

The popularity of these studies made possible a gradual shift in the content and medium of instructional materials particularly after decolonization. In the beginning, textbooks exported to Africa were heavily Eurocentric with only cosmetic changes, for example, supplanting a white face with a black complexion. Irrelevant materials—even in mathematics, generally considered to transcend geographical differences—were rampant.

African governments became fully aware that full freedom and emancipation could only be ensured by regulating what citizens learned. Largely due to nationalist fervor, and in part to awareness of the cosmetic changes made to imported instructional materials, the respective governments took charge of locally publishing more relevant instructional matter. Though relevant curricula true to the realities of respective countries and their development agendas may still be wanting, the conscious effort of national curriculum developers in this respect is commendable.

Numerous deliberations in favor of vernacular languages have been made since independence and particularly since the 1951 UNESCO meeting of experts on the "Use in Education of Indigenous (or Vernacular) Languages and Second Languages, Both in and out of School." In reality, however, the newly independent nations have not been successful yet in implementing these decisions. Breton remarks:

> As far as one can see, more than 30 years since the outset of independence, little has been done for African "national" language development, and the position of European "official" languages is stronger in sub-Saharan Africa [for that matter, most of Africa] than it has ever been before.[19]

As Altbach remarks:

> The work of shifting to an indigenous language is an awesome undertaking. The production of textbooks, the creation of scientific terminology, and a myriad of other obstacles obstruct the emergence of indigenous languages.[20]

Most published materials in Africa—especially the most important textbooks—use metropolitan languages. Textbooks are either imported directly from the West or produced by multinational publishing corporations based locally. Quite a substantial number of textbooks are also published locally by indigenous publishers owned predominantly by respective government bodies and/or parastatals. Nonetheless, these publishers produce western language books that do not help, if not constrain, the growth of African languages, African culture, and the local publishing business.

Unlike other African countries, Ethiopia, was not colonized, and, hence, was not exposed to any external imposition of these metropolitan languages. However, English to a large and French and Italian to a limited extent have been used in the country. English, especially, has been extensively used in schools: it is taught as a subject beginning in grade three and turns into a medium of instruction from grade nine (until recently grade seven) onwards. The medium of instruction in all secondary and higher education institutions has also been English, making it the most important educational language in the country. Although English is widely used in the educational system, as well as many government and nongovernment offices, it would be unrealistic to consider it an important communication medium among the general public. Furthermore, English has had a weak infrastructure upon which to broaden its scope beyond schools in Ethiopia. Good command of English—or, for that matter, other foreign languages—is still primarily a privilege of the few elite who can attend expensive private schools, often affiliated with expatriate community schools.

Ninety-nine languages are spoken in Ethiopia by a population of more than 55 million. The most widely spoken languages are Amharic, Oromigna, and Tigrigna. Historical developments have enabled Amharic to be widely spoken across the country. It was designated as a national language until its status was recently changed to "official language." Amharic is one of the most widely communicated national languages in Africa, with its own unique script and orthography. In Africa, local languages of similar status are very rare.

Is a Designated Vernacular as "Alien" and "Hostile" as a Foreign Language?

Many of the pros and cons of employing foreign languages as a medium of instruction may also hold true for imposed vernacular languages that serve the same purpose. The vernacular languages used as a medium of instruction, however, may be defended on several grounds. First, most vernacular languages have a common historical background and tend to be related in grammatical construction, phonetic structure, and lexicon. Amharic and Tigrigna, for example, belong to the Semitic language group and have close linguistic relationships. Incidentally, all Ethiopian languages generally fall under four groups: Semitic, Cushitic, Omotic, and Nilo-Saharan; Oromigna is the most widely spoken Cushitic language.

Second, vocabularies of vernacular languages widely reflect the common social, cultural, political, psychological, and economic realities of people who have lived together for generations. Using designated national languages thus tends to have a much less alienating impact on the educational process and classroom activity. These designated languages are often spoken widely as either first or second languages.

Third, more people tend to use vernacular languages as a preferred communication medium to foreign languages. In Ethiopia, English is seldom the household communication medium, even of the educated elite; scholars often use local rather than foreign languages for informal and nonofficial communication.

Fourth, the number of national- or regional-based vernacular speakers is much higher than western-based language speakers. For example, while 80 percent of the population in Senegal speaks Wolof, French is spoken by only 15 percent of the population. Yet French enjoys official language status.[21] In Kenya, 75 percent of the books were written in English in 1989, a language inaccessible to 82 percent of the population.[22]

Angola, with a population of 10 million, and Mozambique with 17 million, both have Portuguese as their sole official language, although it is spoken as a mother tongue by only about 1 percent of the population in both countries. In Mozambique, indigenous languages have little formal role.[23]

Whatever the justifications for the use of a national vernacular over a foreign one, efforts are currently underway to provide primary education in vernacular languages throughout the developing world. Countries as far apart as Ghana and Papua New Guinea are actively engaged in the provision of primary education via local languages. Revived concern with the Organization of African Unity's (OAU) 1986 Language Plan of Action for Africa and a growing desire in many countries to move beyond the colonial heritage rather than to replace it jointly favor a new interest in multilingualism and in the language policies and practices being developed in the region.[24]

The next section examines the development of the Ethiopian education system in a historical perspective and reflects on the pros and cons of delegating vernacular languages as media of instruction in primary education. Ethiopia's current initiative to provide primary education in a variety of vernacular languages is examined without dwelling on the broader picture of the campaign pursued by OAU.

Education in Ethiopia: The Ancient, the Recent Past, and the Present

THE ANCIENT

Religious tradition has played a pivotal role in Ethiopian education. Christianity and Islam, and even Judaism and Paganism, have established schools for their followers. In all these schools, religious education was given precedence with the aim of preparing students to assume religious and clerical positions. Christian teaching was dominant in the northern and central regions of the country where the church has exercised its influence since the fourth century A.D. Islam is dominant in the east, south, and west, where Islamic incursions have been frequent and Islam is well entrenched as a religion. The same can be said about Judaism—until the exodus of the *Falashas* (Beth-Israel) very recently—which was limited to the Gondar region, and Paganism, which is confined to the southern, eastern, and western regions of the country. Pagan teaching in particular is based on oral tradition, while education in the other religions draws on both oral and written traditions.[25] It is important to stress that some Ethiopians were literate and sophisticated long before the written word was common currency among the Anglo-Saxons in the British Isles.²⁶

The beginning of church education is difficult to pin down to a date, but the consensus is that it originated in the Kingdom of Axum and reached its most glorious age in Shewa during the period 1200–1500 A.D. The primary aim of church education was to prepare priests, monks, deacons, cantors, and teachers who were mainly expected to render their services to the church. But the church also produced civil servants, judges, governors, scribes, treasurers, and administrators who were employed in the public sector. As there were no other sources of trained manpower prior to the introduction of modern education, most civil servants also assumed the dual responsibility of serving both the church and state. In fact, some of the rulers, such as Zerayacob, were priest-kings.²⁷

Despite the early start of traditional education in Ethiopia, the institutions of learning were constrained by the lack of incentives, physical facilities, and a medium of instruction that could be easily understood by students and teachers. Education was confined to boys, who, after being drilled in the Ethiopian syllabary, passed on to the psalms and then the gospels, which were taught in Ge'ez, a language that neither the teachers nor the students understood very well. However, the rigorous drills in reading and writing served as good discipline, providing the students with a strong base for future education. The same can be said about education in the Koranic schools, which used Arabic, an exotic language with a written script of its own.²⁸ Traditional education lost its significance and dominance after the 1950s with the expansion of modern education.

THE RECENT PAST

As modern education expanded, the influence of the clergy and traditional education declined in significance. This meant that the relationship between the monarchy and the church gradually weakened, opening the way for the emergence of secular education. The Ethiopian military government that seized power in 1974 made major changes in the education system. One of the most significant was ensuring access to education for all. As a result of this policy, thousands of primary and secondary schools were built—primarily through generous Swedish support. The curriculum was blended with a socialist flavor after the government declared its allegiance to the eastern bloc. Through adult education programs, nonformal education was also given special emphasis. Probably one of the most notable achievements of the military regime was its successful adult education program. In 1983, the illiteracy rate was reported to have dramatically dropped from about 90 percent to 37 percent. The government was acclaimed by UNESCO for this outstanding achievement.

The expansion of the formal education system was not, however, commensurate with Ethiopia's material and financial resources. Classes were overcrowded. Textbooks and other instructional materials were in short supply. Teachers carried heavy teaching loads. And the curriculum was cumbersome and to a certain extent irrelevant. All these shortcomings led to a decline in the quality of the education system.

THE PRESENT

A new Ethiopian regime came to power in May 1991 after a long and bloody war. Soon after, it undertook major changes, the most significant being the decentralization of power to regions demarcated along ethnolinguistic lines. A new educational policy was put in place following the creation of a new constitution. In February 1993, Proclamation 45/1985 was promulgated to guarantee the decentralization of decision-making and the division of power between the central and the regional administrations.[29] The most important element of this provision was that each region had the right to use its own language for instruction. Each region was also given responsibility for the provision of primary education (grades one through eight) to its constituency. Section 5.3.1 of the proclamation states that primary education will be given in nationality (local) languages because of the pedagogical advantage of learning in one's mother tongue and the rights of nationalities to promote the use of their languages. Section 5.3.2 stipulates that after making the necessary preparations, nations and nationalities (in the country) can either learn in their own languages or choose from among those selected on the basis of national and country-wide distribution. Consequently, Amharic, the language that had served as a national medium of instruction for more than three decades, was replaced by ethnic languages in most regions. The education system was also changed from a 6+2+4 system to an 8+2+2 system.

As per provision of the proclamation, regional educational bureaus were established. Drafting new curricula and preparation for implementing the new policy started hastily. In fact, some overzealous regions embarked on the new policy before a formal and orderly transition was complete. The speed with which the Oromigna, Wellaytigna, and Sidamgna languages became media of instruction for the entire primary education program strongly indicates the latent interest of the groups, as well as the work already done in these languages during the military regime.[30]

Preparation of Teaching Materials

The role of the central office of the Ministry of Education (MOE) is confined to drafting the general framework of the primary education curricula developed by an assembly of regional educational experts. Regional bureaus have assumed full responsibility for the implementation of the curriculum—developing, transcribing, translating, producing, and distributing instructional materials—once the framework of the curriculum is approved by this assembly. Regions have designated their own trial schools to experiment with the new curriculum before it takes its final form. Syllabi are tested for one year in more than 100 such schools in the country. There are, for example, 26 trial schools in the Oromiya region and five in Region 14.[31]

Writers who develop instructional materials are commissioned by regional educational bureaus. According to a senior officer of a regional bureau, commissioned writers are strongly advised to reflect local realities when developing new instructional materials. These materials are then evaluated by three editors, each focusing on subject matter, language, and pedagogical themes. Once approved, camera-ready copy (CRC) is prepared in-house within the educational bureau and is then delivered to the Educational Materials Production and Distribution Agency (EMPDA) for printing. The officer claims that some encouraging results have been registered since the new system took effect. He attributes, among other improvements, the growth of student population and the increase in some activities of cultural, historical, and language significance to the new initiative.

The quality of curriculum developers, i.e. commissioned writers, varies quite considerably across regions. The Amhara and Tigray regions, in particular, and the Oromiya region, as well, have a comparatively good number of qualified educational experts either as authors or editors with graduate or undergraduate qualifications. However, numerous other smaller groups that have undertaken the provision of primary education in their languages—including the Oromo, the largest group in the country—lack the "critical mass" of literature from which they can choose. This reflects some of the chronic problems that stifle the success of vernacularizing education in most African languages. The Ethiopian experience generally shows that the level of language development, the number of experts working on curriculum development, and the level of preparation to implement language policy vary widely from one vernacular to the other and from one region to another.

The two languages of instructional media used in formal education in

Ethiopia before 1991 were Amharic and English. Amharic was used as a medium of instruction from grade one to grade six, while English was used from grade seven through higher education. Currently, 17 local languages have replaced the area that had been once dominated by Amharic and, to a lesser extent, English. Taking into consideration the vital role played by Amharic still designated as the only "language of countrywide communication"—and Ge'ez, its root, it seems pertinent to provide a brief historical account of their use.

Brief History of Ge'ez and Amharic languages

Ge'ez is considered to be one of the oldest alphabets in the world—perhaps the oldest in Africa—marking Ethiopia's long history of written languages. During the fourth and fifth centuries A.D., when Ethiopia was the center of the trade route to and from the Middle East, Greek was the court language, but Ge'ez was increasingly the language of the people. Inscriptions often used the Ge'ez vernacular. There were Ge'ez versions of the Old and New Testaments.[32] Ge'ez is certainly the first African language into which the Bible was translated.

Ge'ez is believed to be derived from the writing systems of one of the ancient south Arabian languages, probably the Sabean dialect. It consists of a core of 26 letters or characters, each of which occurs in a basic form and in six other forms with diacritic additions representing the vowels, making a total of 182 different characters. Tigrigna uses the same Ge'ez syllabary, while Amharic uses the same characters and eight other basic letters and their diacritically modified forms, representing sounds not found in Ge'ez, thus raising the total number of characters to 238.[33]

As the church became a powerful legitimizing force, Ge'ez became a very important communication medium for the clergy, the royal family, and the people. Written works like the "Book of Psalms" and "The Song of Songs" were printed in Ge'ez in Rome and Cologne in the early sixteenth century. A Ge'ez translation of the New Testament was printed in Rome in 1548.[34]

As the Axumite Empire gradually declined, Amharic replaced Ge'ez. Though Amharic successfully displaced Ge'ez in social, cultural, political, and economic life, Ge'ez took refuge in the traditional Coptic orthodox churches and monasteries, which have changed very little, if at all, for generations. Today, Ge'ez is still very much a traditional part of the strong Orthodox church within Ethiopia.

Although Amharic was recognized as the language of the court as early as 1270, and some Amharic manuscripts from the fourteenth and seventeenth centuries were extant, it was not until the reign of Emperor

Tewodros II (1855–1868) that Amharic literature achieved full recognition. Under Tewodros' rule, Amharic was given the greatest encouragement as a language of literature and national unification.[35] The movement of Amharic-speaking people at the end of the nineteenth and the beginning of the twentieth century to the east, south, and west, coupled with the aspiration of successive rulers to create a monolithic Ethiopian Empire, played a major role in the spread of Amharic. As Amharic was later elevated to a medium of instruction in all primary schools, it widened its scope and became legitimized.

Because Amharic has been used in schools and has served as a language of formal and nonformal communication, it is widely spoken, read, written, and published. Amharic, which uses the Ge'ez script, has one very prominent advantage over other languages that use Latin script. Ge'ez uses a phonetic system of spelling in which each sound is represented by one written symbol and each written symbol represents one sound. Problems of orthography—spelling and standardization—are remarkably minimized as a result. Notably, Ge'ez uses a smaller number of letters in representing words as opposed to Latin scripts, which can be excessive, depending on the complexity of the language and the caliber of experts involved.

Many of the regional education experts that opted for the Latin script, however, allege that the Ge'ez script provides limited opportunity and flexibility for exploiting electronic and information technologies. They further argue that Ge'ez script has its own limitations—even for Amharic—and the decision to adopt Latin script was to avoid these problems. This is part of the controversy of multilingual education in Ethiopia and will be discussed later.

Teaching Material Production Profile for the New Curriculum

The production of new instructional materials in vernacular languages for primary schools started along two parallel lines: one from grade one (for basic education) and the other from grade five (for general education). Each year, two grades (one from each level) have been added. Many regional bureaus have recruited native experts to work on the new teaching materials.

Experts review the curriculum based on the educational policy, which stipulates that the curriculum should be developed and textbooks prepared on sound pedagogical and psychological principles and international standards, giving due attention to concrete local conditions and gender issues. This policy, according to a regional educational chief, not only fosters the production of a sound curriculum, but also facilitates the elimination of some culturally offensive materials from the curriculum.

Another senior educational expert, however, laments that some less-privileged regions stand in more precarious and disadvantaged positions today, as they failed to fill up vacant teacher positions that were created by the new initiative. These regions had to grapple with a lack of capable expertise for this task that would shape the destiny of their citizens. Even where some experts were present, it has been reported that their contributions have been curtailed by political bickering, favoritism, and isolation. Implementing primary education in vernacular languages is also likely to be fraught with acrimony, particularly in those regions where there are many competing languages and cultural groups. The Southern Nations, Nationalities, and Peoples Region (SNNPR) which is divided into nine zones, for example, has to deal with several dozen languages.

The Predicament of Teacher Training Institutions

The medium of instruction in teacher training institutions (TTIs) was originally English. But the provisions of the proclamation Section 3.5.2 stipulate that "The language of teacher training for kindergarten and primary education will be the nationality language used in the area," so English was replaced by numerous vernacular languages. On the surface, this move appeared to have resolved the problem of training in English and teaching in Amharic. Many problems, however, soon cropped up. It became apparent that teachers trained in one region in one vernacular language would become the responsibility of that particular region and must be absorbed by it. This not only limits the movement of teachers across regions, but also impinges on their marketability.

In the academic arena, many TTI graduates were reported to have found the new curriculum, terminologies, and medium of instruction difficult. This difficulty is not restricted to the newly emerged vernacular languages of instruction. Some senior educational experts in MOE and elsewhere agree that some of the Amharic words introduced in the curriculum feel "exotic" even to them. In areas of some syllabi, widespread inconsistency became apparent in the regions. Some regions insisted that they start Amharic at the basic level, while others introduced it at the second phase. Some regions, such as SNNPR and Gambella, have had to grapple with several languages, while others, such as Amhara, Oromo, and Tigray, had to deal with only one. In those regions where many languages bear equal importance and the composition of nonnative groups is large, some classes or even schools had to be set aside to satisfy the major groups. This entailed not only the adoption of different curricula and languages in one region but in one school compound. Consequently, this inevitably drives cost and complicates the educational programs—including the TTIs—in those ethnically diverse regions that are considered to be historically underprivileged.

The Transition to Vernacular Languages and the Controversy of Designating Scripts

The issue of teaching in vernacular languages in Ethiopia has been further complicated by controversy over designating scripts. Amharic, Tigrigna, and Guragigna use the Ge'ez script. All the groups that have chosen to use the Ge'ez script belong to the Semitic group. Some Semitic groups that initially decided to use Latin script have now reverted to Ge'ez script. Benshangul-Gumuz, which is a non-Semitic group, uses the Ge'ez script. Addis Ababa (Region 14) uses the Amharic language and the Ge'ez script, as does the Amhara Region (Region 3). In some schools that cater to different ethnic groups, both scripts are being used.

The largest non-Semitic ethnic group that decided to use the Latin script is the Oromiya Region (Region 4). Many Oromo scholars contend that the Latin script is more appropriate for the Oromo language than the Ge'ez script. They further argue that Ge'ez script has its shortcomings, even for Amharic—the major beneficiary of the script. Numerous other ethnic languages have also opted to use the Latin script. Many critics point out, however, that the decision to designate a script has also been politically motivated. When a high-ranking educational officer was asked to substantiate the grounds upon which the "more appropriate script for his language" was chosen, he simply responded: "You do not need research for everything; natural observation dictates action." Politics seems to be generally pervasive in language policy decisions. Woodhall points out that some researchers involved in a study on five African countries found that language policy is regarded as politically sensitive and officials or teachers were not always willing to discuss their experiences frankly. Hence, what actually happens in schools does not always conform with official policy declarations.[36]

The Latin script that replaced Ge'ez appears to have suffered from one major problem. Due to a largely overzealous effort, the transcribed Latin words have become excessively long. Moreover, as of yet, there is a lack of conventional orthography for most of the new instructional languages. This may have an impact on the achievement of primary schoolchildren who have to deal with two scripts—Latin first and Ge'ez later. It is worrisome that this same problem affects not only the schoolchildren, but also their TTI-graduated teachers.

Many nationalists, scholars, and opposition groups vehemently condemn the decision to use Latin script as much as they oppose abandoning Amharic as the medium of instruction. They disregard the changes in the education system as some of the political tactics of the minority government to stay in power. Some even argue that the current language policy is a replica of the same strategy used in apartheid South Africa, which not only promoted Afrikaans as the language of the ruling minority but encouraged the use of so-called tribal languages, such as Setswana, Sesotho, Khosa, and Zulu, in pursuit of a divide-and-rule policy.[37] Other critics argue that if the ruling elite was not fueled by divisive intent, the transition would have been less chaotic and gradual. They charge that the initiative is a conscious plot by the minority ruling elite to attenuate the sphere of dominance of its historical rivals. They also regret that while most of the Third World and Africa is talking about "displacing colonial languages in favor of their own," Ethiopia's current practice is contrary to this initiative.

The accusations of critics and opponents of the current policy may not be totally groundless. The ruling party was in pursuit of vernacularization long before the infrastructure was in place. Instructional materials were poorly prepared; competent teachers familiar with vernacular languages were not available; and the infrastructure was not receptive when the new scheme was launched. Regardless of the views of proponents and opponents, the overall initiative was poorly and hastily implemented.

Whatever the motives, replacing the Ge'ez script with the Latin script for numerous languages has undoubtedly annulled much of the achievements of the 17-year nonformal literacy campaign based on the Ge'ez script. A very high percentage of the adult population that was claimed to have become literate may relapse to illiteracy largely because of the change from the Ge'ez to Latin script.

Linguists and educational psychologists agree that the use of the mother tongue as a language of instruction in the early years of education has proven advantages, especially the development of cognitive faculties. Conversely, it has been demonstrated that classroom use of a language that is not the language already spoken by the child results in cognitive and pedagogical difficulties.[38] Cognizant of this fact, many countries in Africa and Asia provide primary education in mother tongues; this is not peculiar to Ethiopia. In India, for example, 50 of the 96 living languages qualify for the status of written languages, since all "50 languages are used as mediums for primary schooling in different parts of the country."[39] In one of the most culturally and linguistically diverse nations in the Asia-Pacific region, Papua New Guinea, 44 percent of the 815 living languages have alphabets designed for them and 33 percent have some books produced in that language. Ghana is also a highly diverse community with numerous languages; it has been developing its various vernacular languages, about 15 of which have already been transcribed.[40] In all of these initiatives, we witness a considerable emphasis on designing a realistic time table for transition. For example, since 1989, Papua New Guinea has been steadily moving toward implementing education reform, which includes the use of the children's vernacular language as the language of instruction in the elementary years of schooling. Implementation of the reform throughout the nation will be a gradual process, taking ten years or more.[41] A Senegalese Deputy Minister in charge of Basic Education and National Languages affirms that, "Moving from an oral to a written language is not a spontaneous process. There needs to be research and decisions taken to transcribe oral languages."[42]

What makes the Ethiopian case problematic is the manner in which it has been chaotically and poorly implemented. The Ethiopian initiative for vernacularizing primary education should learn a lot not only from the successes but the failures of others that have already experimented with similar initiatives. It could learn a lot, for example, from Guinea, a country that suspended its vernacularization program in 1984 in favor of French. Their many reasons included: lack of preparation of parents and teachers; lack of previous experimentation; lack of teacher training in new methodologies; and lack of appropriate support for teaching in six languages, all characteristic symptoms of the Ethiopian case.[43]

Bloor and Tamrat argue that the effect of the new curriculum in Ethiopia is to boost English at the expense of Amharic. They reflect the view of contemporary scholars working in the field of language planning who bemoan the lack of status of indigenous African languages, which are increasingly losing out to colonial languages in their view.[44] Amharic, however, appears to be too deeply rooted in the economic, social, political, religious, and cultural functions of the people to loose its significance easily. The author thus does not share the concern of these scholars regarding the fate of Amharic.

Communication barriers abound in regional offices that use the newly designated vernaculars and also Latin script. One scholar said, "life would be easier if we can use the familiar old script" to enhance the gains already made using our own language. Many also agree that words are excessively long and lack standardized form, causing confusion and frustration. A senior regional educational officer admits the presence of such "minor" problems of standardization in his region, where there are numerous dialects. He was optimistic that the inclusion of glossaries in textbooks would solve many of these problems, and hopes that the problems may eventually dissipate as students, teachers, and the society familiarize themselves with the new changes.

The Ethiopian experience with multilingual education is not only constrained by the proliferation of languages and the acrimony over the selection of scripts. It is also complicated by numerous dialects, particularly in widely spoken languages. Producing a textbook using a dialect from one group may not be satisfying to others. An educational expert indicated that the educational office attempts to ensure the composition of editors from major dialect groups to address this concern.

The division of regions and zones along ethnolinguistic lines, despite all its proclaimed merits, has some shortcomings, too. While the big regions have to deal with only one language, others such as SNNPR have to grapple with more than a dozen. SNNPR accounts for about half of the total ethnic groups of the country. Currently, five working languages have been designated in this nine-zone region. To complicate matters, this region has a serious shortage of trained personnel to deal with the current initiative, except probably in a few languages such as Guragigna, Sidamigna, and Kembatgna.

For a region like SNNPR, the task of producing a variety of instructional materials for all the groups under its jurisdiction is an enormous, challenging, and costly undertaking. The cost of preparing textbooks is much higher for this region than those that have to deal with only one language. According to one estimate, a book that has a unit cost of one for one million copies in a single language costs as much as 16.7 for the same number of copies in ten languages. In addition to having few trained and capable teachers and educators in the region, the high cost incurred in the preparation such a of variety of instructional materials undoubtedly drains much of the educational budget of these regions. It also appears that these regions do not enjoy substantial support for dealing with such nuances. For example, the budget allocated to Region 3—with one vernacular language—is equivalent to SNNPR's—a region that has to deal with nine such languages and, very interestingly, also caters to twice as many students.

Reports indicate that the process of translating and transcribing curricular materials has also not been isolated from politics. One bureau chief admitted that his team would not coin or adopt any words from other vernacular languages, even when these words do not exist in his language. He firmly underscored that he would rather create a new word than legitimize the already adopted words from other local languages.

Needless to say, some languages have developed more than others for various historical reasons. Even highly developed international languages, such as English, have many words borrowed from other languages. It appears pathetic, if not ignorant, to contemplate the creation of a "pure" language with no elements from other language groups. Lack of broad knowledge in language development fused with misguided political interests and shallow arguments may consequently affect the interests of millions of people.

The argument here is not to revert to the past, but for the new initiatives to be based on critical, careful, responsible, and, "apolitical" argument. For sure, the task of implementing school instruction policy in a multitude of vernacular languages, even for economically and technologically privileged countries, is a challenging one. Ethiopia, an economically poor country, is home to a diverse people with 99 languages. Of these, about 20 percent are currently used as a medium of instruction. Despite the shortcomings that have plagued the initiative, it is still a commendable effort.

According to Daswani:

> For a language to qualify for written status, it is essential that there should exist in that language a reasonable body of printed literature by native speakers of the language and that the language should be the medium of instruction in the primary school. The use of the language as the medium of instruction in the primary schools is an important criterion since it promotes language development and standardization because it leads to the writing of textbooks and other literature of information.[45]

The usage of vernaculars as media of instruction is well underway in Ethiopia. What remains to be done is the big task—and challenge—of developing a body of literature for most of these languages; otherwise, citizens may relapse to illiteracy. Many regions are conscious of this impending danger; some have undertaken measures such as organizing literature contests between schools to generate materials. According to an Oromiya educational officer, such contests take place between the 2,500 schools in the region. About 130 selected materials in six volumes have been produced, published, and distributed to all schools in the region since this initiative was launched.

Glamorizing vernacularization and promoting the cultural heritage of a nation does not come without a price. Many African countries face the complexities and challenges of serving a multilingual and multicultural society. The prohibitive cost of implementing the policy of vernacularizing schools and shortage of trained personnel may force many African countries to act slowly and carefully. Even South Africa, a country with a relatively strong economy, faces the practical difficulties of entertaining 11 official languages.

Parallel with this initiative, governments should also be encouraged to courageously promote selected native languages to national and/or official status to enhance communication. In the absence of a strong communication link, minority groups may be marginalized and isolated further. As much as the effort to provide primary education in local languages is underscored, emphasis should also be made to promote native languages widely spoken in a country. Tanzania, a country of 120 languages, for example, emphasizes the provision of primary education in the Kiswahili language. Kiswahili is not only a national language, but a regional communication medium widely spoken in Uganda and Kenya. Namibia has given "national" status to 13 local languages.[46] In Ethiopia, educational policy stipulates that Amharic and English should be taught in all primary schools. The practice, however, has been inconsistent across its regions.

Where Do We Go from Here?

Many languages known only in oral form were transformed in less than two years to a written one, in a less organized manner. The transition could have been better had it not been for the elements of politics that often plague such issues. Negash observes that campaign-flavored policy implementation characteristic of Ethiopian political history unfortunately prevailed again, hijacking what could have been an encouraging effort in promoting language, culture, and heritage.[47]

It is reprehensible to abandon the fate of millions of schoolchildren to incompetent, poorly qualified, and biased personnel on the pretext of autonomy and self-administration. The central government should act quickly, responsibly, and actively to ensure that regional administrations execute their duties meticulously, responsibly, and competently. The current disparity that exists between regions in terms of trained personnel not only undermines the prospect of students from the historically underprivileged regions, but may also broaden the existing rifts between regions. Recently, the prime minister officially recognized these problems and indicated that some "regional governments [that] are not as capable [of]" are being aided by the government.[48] Augmenting regional activities through cautious involvement of the central government may promote the policies of the federal and regional governments.

To maintain and ensure the integrity, consistency, and quality of the education system throughout the country, all the regions work from the same skeleton curriculum developed by Institute of Curriculum Development and Research (ICDR), a central government body. But the significance of this effort may be attenuated as it is pushed and pulled around in different directions at different levels by scholars of varying academic stature. A huge discrepancy in expertise, competency, and material resources exists between regions from the time the framework of the curriculum is being reviewed to the next phase of development—writing, translating, and transcribing instructional materials.

The task of translating and transcribing vernacular languages that have as yet developed practically no reference materials, dictionaries, or a significant body of literature is an arduous one. It requires, among others, a critical mass of experts executing their duties competently, carefully, and responsibly from a wide array of disciplines. In a situation in which major decisions are dictated by less competent politicians of limited political scope, the consequences may be detrimental to the same people the government strives to promote. The hasty and chaotic implementation of the current policy may not only frustrate present and undermine future efforts, it may have grave consequences as well.

Regional educational bureaus should be encouraged to work together, freely discuss common problems, candidly air out their views, and propose pragmatic solutions. They should also involve language institutions, scholars, and lay people in their work. Regions self- sufficient in human resources should be encouraged to work closely with and support needy ones. They also should assess their activities carefully, regularly, and actively; immediate measures have to be taken to alleviate problems encountered. The role of the central government in realizing this is very crucial. This should not, however, be construed as advocating the reinstatement of centralization through another door. It is the responsibility of the central government to see to it that educational policy, for that matter any policy, is implemented effectively, efficiently, carefully, competently, and equitably in all regions. This requires a healthy political will, good vision, and responsible personnel.

The most critical responsibility of any educational system in the Third World, and Africa in particular, is ensuring the provision of textbooks and other instructional materials. Textbooks, in particular, play a vital role in these countries, where other reading materials and sources of information are in very short supply. The next section examines the production and publication of textbooks and other instructional materials against the background of the new educational policy.

Textbook Publishing in the Ethiopian Education System

Ethiopia is one of the African countries with a poor publishing infrastructure. Unlike other African countries whose publishing infrastructure has been shaped by western colonial rulers, the Ethiopian publishing enterprise is basically a home-grown initiative.

In 1898, the first printing house was founded in the capital by Emperor Menelik II. It produced the first regular periodicals, pamphlets, and newspapers, as well as some original literary and historical works, philosophical and religious treatises, and hymnals and chronicles.[49] A small book production center for primary education was established in 1957, marking the beginning of textbook production under the authority of the Ministry of Education. The period from 1962 to 1972 witnessed the printing and distribution of additional primary school textbooks that had been translated and adopted from a series produced in English.[50] Until the 1974 revolution, private publishers, such as Oxford University Press, had a minor publishing operation, particularly in English textbooks. Multinationals failed to dominate the local market by importing school materials as they did elsewhere. This was because, first, the language of instruction in primary schools was Amharic; and, second, the student population in secondary and tertiary education that predominantly relied on imported books was then very small.

In a major education policy shift, the military regime in post-1974 revolutionary Ethiopia was highly involved in ensuring universal primary education, emphasizing adult education, designing relevant curricula, and overhauling the entire education system. As part of the effort to meet these requirements, the need to establish a state-owned publishing organization became clear. An organization that later became known as Educational Materials Production and Distribution Agency (EMPDA) was established in 1975–76 with significant Swedish funds, through SIDA and its personnel. Over the years, particularly during the military regime, SIDA became the largest bilateral donor to the education sector in terms of school construction and textbook production.

EMPDA was established to address the following objectives:

- to publish students' textbooks, teachers' guides, reference materials, charts and maps, etc.;
- to produce school furniture, science, technical, vocational, and other educational equipment, and erect, repair, and maintain them;
- to purchase educational materials—locally and from abroad—and distribute them to different regions in the country; and

- to carry out research necessary for the improvement and increased production of educational materials.

Textbooks and other instructional materials were published centrally by MOE until decentralization took effect in post-1991 Ethiopia. The curriculum was centrally developed and books were centrally published in two languages—Amharic and English—by the ICDR. The books were printed by EMPDA—the major publisher, printer, and distribution agency of the central government—or subcontracted to four other printers that operated under the now defunct Ethiopian Printing Corporation. When one spoke of local textbook production and publishing in the country, one generally talked until very recently about the pros and cons of publishing in this organization.

In addition to its major responsibilities in textbook production, EMPDA has been involved in the provision of science kits and furniture for schools. The cost of machinery and printing paper has been generously supported by SIDA. The support of SIDA to EMPDA amounts to more than 60 million Swedish kroner in the form of printing facilities, training, and paper.[51] EMPDA is still the sole producer of textbooks for all the regions. For example, during 1993–94 alone, EMPDA had the technical capacity to print up to 5 million textbooks in more than 10 languages.[52]

One of the major attractions of EMPDA has been especially the low cost of textbook and other instructional material production. Cost of production and printing at EMPDA has been cheaper compared to other private and commercial printing presses because paper is either supplied for free by SIDA or heavily subsidized by the government. SIDA has been the major source of paper for EMPDA. Paper has been subsidized or freely supplied for EMPDA.

Regional educational bureaus are now responsible for producing, publishing, printing, and distributing textbooks and other instructional materials and deal directly with the agency. Interacting with numerous regional education or other bureau officials, who are usually political appointees and almost always unaware of the art of book production, has become a challenging experience, particularly in terms of maintaining production schedules. Currently EMPDA deals with numerous regional educational bureaus and many other high-ranking authorities. This may constrain the agency from executing its duties professionally, given the lack of awareness of book production requirements among many in power. Reports indicate that regional bureau officials compete for priority. This could easily turn into a political scenario in which some regions get instructional materials and others do not.

One may wonder what the future may hold for EMPDA in light of the central government's current policy of withdrawing its support from such public institutions and encouraging them to become self-sufficient. Current policies of donor agencies do not seem to support the hegemony of EMPDA in the textbook market, either. These policies emphasize shifting the support from the producer to the consumer. Though the central government seems to be firm in liberalizing the economy—currently about 200 government-owned institutions have been privatized—some bigger regions were contemplating the establishment of their own region-based EMPDAs.

EMPDA's current annual production has now reached 6.5 million. The agency now functions in three shifts, producing instructional materials in 17 different vernacular languages. In 1995–96, it produced 5,191,193 copies in-house and 2,458,276 copies by subcontracting with other printers. According to Terefe, a total of nearly 37.5 million books produced by EMPDA were distributed between 1987–88 and 1994–95.[53] EMPDA currently subcontracts about 10 major printing houses in the capital, including the oldest printing press, Berhanena Selam, Artistic, Bole, and Central Printing Enterprises. The agency supplies paper to subcontractors and bidders for free.

Until September 1996, more than 900 different instructional materials were produced in 17 vernacular languages, including Afar, Agnwak, Amharic, Benshangul-Gumuz, Dawrogna, Gedeogna, Hadiygna, Harari, Keftcho, Kembatgna, Oromigna, Sidamgna, Somaligna, Tigrigna, and Wollaytgna.[54] Efforts are in full swing to add more languages to this list. During the previous regime, according to McNab, about 400 titles were on the publication lists of EMPDA for formal and nonformal education.[55]

As long as the present arrangement of free paper provision or special treatment by way of heavy subsidy to EMPDA remains, regions will continue to be drawn to the agency. As the variety and quantity of books increase—owing to the growing student population and the increased number of languages used for primary education—the capacity and capability of EMPDA to produce these materials may become limited.

With the consistent and generous support of external funding agencies, particularly SIDA, EMPDA has managed to cope with demand until now. Parallel with the government's policy of decentralization and regionalization, NGOs have started working closely with regional bureaus. Some regional education bureaus, for example, have already started tendering bids directly for the publication and printing of instructional materials using the financial and technical support of NGOs. This development appears to have opened the opportunity for private publishers and printers to compete in the market and promote self-sufficiency of respective regional education bureaus. The success and sustainability of this development, however, largely depends on careful management and responsible, competent, and trustworthy personnel in the regional bureaus.

External organizations that operate in the general area of publishing include the Finnish Development Organization, German Development Programs (DVV and GTZ), UNDP, UNICEF, and USAID. The support from these and other NGOs to regional educational bureaus has increased as the government has mounted pressure on these agencies to streamline their programs in terms of the national development policy. The policy of USAID—one of the most active current foreign aid participants in the Ethiopian education system—concurs with the view of the recent government regionalization policy that efforts to strengthen the primary education system should strongly emphasize building infrastructure in the regions. This generally illustrates the NGOs' growing center of focus. Should SIDA decide to follow others and redirect its support to regions, EMPDA— a national institution—may face financial and technical difficulties. However, until most of the regions find alternative means to produce their instructional materials, which seems to appear unlikely in the near future, it is hoped that support to the agency from the government and NGOs will continue.

Given the growing variety and quantity of instructional materials, relying on and supporting one agency alone may not be realistic, productive, or appropriate. One indication of this challenge is reflected in the Summary Report by the evaluation team of the Try Out Project that assessed the activities of designated schools pioneering vernacular education.[56] One of the reasons for the delay in launching the Try Out schools was late delivery of instructional materials, for which EMPDA was allegedly responsible. In Oromiya, the region that houses the greatest number of Try Out schools in the country, the launching of the program was delayed by one to five months.

Officials at EMPDA, however, strongly deny these charges. They direct responsibility for the problem back to the regional educational personnel who, they claim, have very limited knowledge of book publishing, and hence, did not allow enough time for textbook preparation. One senior expert at EMPDA lamented that some regional officials expect a book to be produced, printed, and distributed in two months!

Whatever the arguments, there is a great need for more publishing institutions and printing houses in the country. As much as it has played a prominent role in the history of Ethiopian education, EMPDA has also overshadowed the emergence of indigenous private publishing enterprises;

in fact, the policy of the previous regime was anti-privatization. The publishing industry now stands at a crossroads. EMPDA should give up its hegemony in the area of textbook production—the cream of the publishing industry in the Third World, and Africa in particular—so that other private publishers might emerge. The attempt to replicate EMPDA in the regions may not foster the development of the national publishing industry. Doing so would not only stunt the growth of a strong private publishing industry, but would appear to countervail the current government policy of privatization and commercialization.

Ethiopia, unlike most of the rest of black Africa, has had a history of "independent" publishing, with minimal interest from multinational corporations. It has an estimated population of more than 55 million, with an annual population growth rate of three percent—about 50 percent below 15 years of age. This calls for a larger, more vibrant publishing institutions. Opening up the business of textbook and other instructional material production could not be more timely.

The responsibility of the government now lies in fostering the emergence of many indigenous and collaborative ventures by promulgating policies on, *inter alia*, tax relief, tax exemption, and the provision of bank loans for publishers. Before dismantling the existing infrastructure, the government has to ensure that the new approach works well and is sustainable, particularly for the sake of those smaller and highly diverse regions that may not be considered viable publishing customers by private entrepreneurs.

What draws regional bureaus to EMPDA is not its cheap production cost alone. EMPDA has the capacity, capability, long experience, and, above all, concerned expertise to make textbooks. Many regional educational bureau officials agree that EMPDA has a concern for quality in production and content of the material. Substandard CRC materials are either frequently returned to their producers in the respective regional bureaus or, most of the time, have to be "polished" at the premises of the agency. According to an EMPDA expert, it is very rare to find materials that could go into print directly without requiring some expert attention. Furthermore, on its premises, EMPDA provides group-working facilities and publishing guidance for educational experts from the regions.

It appears that EMPDA has now diversified its role over the years since the 1991 government change. This includes liasing with regions on curriculum issues; providing technical advice and expertise in publishing; initiating training and workshops; and providing free consultancy to all regions. The creation of a forum at the premises of the agency that brought together various regional experts has been instrumental in establishing close working relationships between regional educational bureaus. This enabling environment also has the following advantages:

- It is cost effective. Regional educational bureau officials, for example, will be trained on the cost ineffectiveness of putting in orders for very small—as little as 10- or 20-copy—print runs, which has been the case on many occasions.
- It creates a forum to exchange views, opinions, and experiences and to deal with common challenges across regional boundaries. It also helps to develop trust between regional educational bureaus and the agency.
- It facilitates the search for collective solutions to common problems and enables immediate collective recommendations regarding regional and national problems that frequently crop up.
- It fosters consistency and better monitoring standards in the nation's educational system amidst the diversity of curricula and instructional materials.
- It allows representatives of regional educational bureaus to focus primarily on their jobs. The physical detachment from their respective regions exempts them from social, political, as well as other official responsibilities, enabling them to concentrate their time and energy on their work.
- Most importantly, it creates awareness of the production and publication of textbooks. This awareness will eventually spread, it is hoped, to higher authorities that will promote the whole publication effort.

In order to cut the outrageous expense of printing very small print runs, some experts in education and publishing advise certain regions to develop their duplicating and copying capabilities. They contend that some regions will probably have to use photocopying or simple duplicating machines instead of employing conventional printing presses. Taking heed of this professional advice would best serve some regions that require a small print run, thus avoiding exorbitant unit costs on certain books that, for example, cost more than 100 birr.[57] The unit costs for books vary enormously by regions. For example, while a teachers' guide costs between 2 birr and 12.05 birr in Oromiya, the figure for some books, such as the Sports and Physical Education Teachers' Guide for the Gambella Region, exceeds 100 birr.

Oromo are the largest ethnic group in the country. They also have the highest number of schools, students, and teachers. The region thus produces instructional materials in bulk; hence the smaller per unit cost of a book. As the print run for each vernacular grows smaller, the unit cost grows higher. Economies of scale thus still favor those languages with large numbers of students and teachers. If a book has to be purchased, students in the smaller regions are at a disadvantage if the cost becomes unrealistically expensive—something that may have serious consequences on these regions.

One of the most serious problems facing current educational policy on textbook provision is the complexity of the process by which books are produced and distributed. Formerly, this was done on the basis of a set ratio of students to books by MOE through EMPDA. Currently, educational bureaus order books based on the budget earmarked to them by their respective regions. This practice may undermine the effort of ensuring book provision for those schoolchildren who live in regions that have to grapple with numerous vernacular languages.

Furthermore, accurate and reliable data on student enrollment by language of instruction is not easy to obtain. Often data are either deliberately inflated or nonexistent. The fact that the bureaucratic echelon of the new education system has increased by one level does not seem to help either. Particularly in a situation in which political consciousness is high and zones within regions have to compete for budgets, the education program may be undermined further. For example, in SNNPR, where there are nine zones and numerous vernacular language groups, the situation could be further constrained by poor infrastructure and management of book distribution. The higher the number and variety of textbooks produced in different vernaculars for a region, the more complex and more expensive, as well as more error-prone, the distribution and management may be.

One of the weaknesses of the current publishing scene in Ethiopia is the absence of a national book policy. A national book policy that carefully, broadly, and clearly addresses those issues that promote indigenous publishing in the private sector is needed. Particularly for the current initiative regarding multilingual education to bear fruit, private indigenous publishing initiatives should be vigorously promoted. The presence of a functional national book policy not only fosters the textbook market but nurtures the general publishing infrastructure of a country. It is encouraging to note that preliminary work is underway to institute a national book policy.

The Ethiopian publishing landscape has been punctuated by various forces and events. The educational policy of the current government—and the former government to some extent—has made possible the provision of various instructional materials in multiple vernacular languages.

The promulgation of press freedom by the current government caused an avalanche of privately owned publications and has rekindled the state of publishing in the country. It is beyond the scope of this chapter to deliberate on this development.

Conclusions and Recommendations

The practice of multilingual education and publishing in Ethiopia started during the Mengistu era. At that time, the national literacy campaign in nonformal education was using 15 different vernacular languages. Few schools were also designated in some regions as experimental and used local languages as the medium of instruction. What makes the current initiative different and bold is that it clearly and unequivocally spells out the language policy in the Constitution vis-à-vis its relationship with primary education. The proclamation clearly states that, by making the necessary preparations, nations and nationalities can either learn in their own languages or choose from among those selected on the basis of national and country-wide distribution.

We have, however, witnessed a hasty and less-organized implementation of the policy. Drawing from the experience of other countries that have embarked on the provision of education in local languages, such initiatives should be executed gradually. For the realization of pedagogical and psychological benefits that may accrue from instruction in one's mother tongue, adequate preparation for developing better instructional materials and a body of literature, the upgrading of often poorly trained primary school teachers, and more pragmatic approaches to the initiative, beyond rhetoric, are strongly needed. It is, however, naive to think that language policy decisions are based merely on pedagogic and psychological factors; they are highly contentious issues fraught with politics, economics, and self-interest.

Policy issues and decisions on the use of vernacular languages as a medium of instruction may not bring about immediate changes in either educational performance or cognitive development, despite what many politicians would like to see. They have to realize that the policies could be frustrated and constrained at various levels, including textbook and instructional material production and distribution, the quality and preparedness of school teachers to teach in the new languages, the commitment of school and regional administrations to involve themselves in the campaign, and the willingness of students and their families to freely participate in the program. Neither the success nor the weakness of the program should be unduly inflated, nor failures ignored or hidden. Likewise, critics should neither exaggerate weaknesses or failures nor misconstrue the measured or perceived results.

It may be an extremely expensive undertaking—or may even be impractical in the foreseeable future—to provide education in all vernacular languages of the country. Particularly those regions that have been considered as underprivileged (and, by coincidence, that also have several languages) may have to consider seriously the cost and complexity of this mammoth task. The educational budget allocated to Region 3, which deals with only one language, for example, is approximately equivalent to that of SNNPR, which has to grapple with nine languages and also twice as many students. Should all the regions, zones, and districts pursue the initiative aggressively and in haste—as has happened for the last couple of years—they may eventually force their own groups to be marginalized farther from the center of the economic, social, and political power base. Furthermore, in those regions that cater to more than one language, the issue of distributing and allocating the often meager budget and other resources among them may likely be an acrimonious one that has a detrimental impact on both education and the development of the region, and the whole nation in general.

As it stands now, most students at the elementary level will continue to be confronted with three languages: the designated native language, Amharic, and English. To make matters worse, these students also have to deal with two, or even more, different scripts. This may undermine the pedagogical benefits envisaged in the proclamation regarding education in vernacular languages.

It is fair to assume, though, that the central government and especially the regional political bodies may have neither the financial leverage nor the infrastructure to provide education in all the languages spoken in the country. The provision of education in a vernacular language may eventually be dictated by the location and number of speakers in a particular region and the economic realities associated with it. For example, while SNNPR caters to numerous languages, the Oromo, Amhara, and Tigray regions—those that have relatively better infrastructure and management—deal with only one each. SNNPR, and other regions as well, may need to reconsider the implementation of the policy now that they have already taken on more than they could effectively handle. Following from this, it would be pragmatic to designate certain widely spoken regional languages as media of instruction and develop the rest gradually by building infrastructure and drawing on the experience of the past.

A genuine, open, critical, and all-encompassing forum for debate that could disentangle emotional and political vagaries from realities is crucial to the success of efforts to vernacularize education. The debate should focus not only on the benefits and potentials that may accrue from vernacularizing primary education, but the costs, consequences, and sacrifices that may have to be made. The move of some of the regions to critically review their performance is encouraging.

Amharic should be strongly emphasized beginning at the lower primary level to benefit all students, including those who may have to drop out of school early. This will help create an opportunity and means for the nation to speak one common language while diversifying the others. A nation needs one common, widely spoken language—a national *lingua franca*. While other vernacular languages could be promoted, the role of Amharic—the language that binds the nation together—should not be underestimated. Ethiopia should learn from the experience of other countries.

Amharic, though not comparable with the breadth and strength of other international and regional languages such as Kiswahili, still has many speakers all over the country. Precluding any ethnic or language group from learning Amharic may be tantamount to denying a group from actively participating in economic, social, and political affairs of the nation. The effort to advance one's language should not prompt the displacement of another—particularly an important and widely established national language like Amharic. Thinking locally *and* acting nationally should be the premise on which decisions regarding national languages rest.

Easy access to published materials plays a profound role in the success and sustainability of the current initiative. A large sum of quality books are required to strengthen the current initiative. Unless the newly literate are provided with relevant reading materials, they may relapse into illiteracy. Regional educational administrations should be encouraged to be more self-reliant in the publication of more books and reading materials in the newly introduced media of instruction. In the absence of literature and reading materials, and given the shortage of textbooks and expertise, the danger of relapsing into illiteracy is imminent. To mitigate this danger, regional offices and the central government should encourage authors to develop new and relevant materials, publishers to publish in these vernaculars, and donors to support such programs.

It is important that research in codification, orthography, and standardization be promoted in all the languages used in the provision of education in vernacular languages. As Wagaw warns, "Until such work in African languages reaches an adequate level, the efforts of African states to foster the utilization of African mother tongues and national languages, and the preservation and promotion of cultures and traditions will remain elusive."[58] Equally important, decisions—especially those based on critical analysis and reliable data—should not be biased or manipulated for political or other purposes.

The language and educational policies of Ethiopia appear to lack a very important component that is crucial for their implementation and strength. Like most African countries, Ethiopia has yet to promulgate a national book policy. This national book policy, when it comes into existence, should take into account other related policies, as well as the regional discrepancies and capabilities in book production and distribution discussed in this chapter.

Indigenous private publishers should be strongly encouraged to participate actively in this initiative, currently dominated by government institutions such as EMPDA. EMPDA has done an outstanding job not only publishing instructional materials for schools all over the country, but also making possible the publication of numerous other academic books. Today, EMPDA stands at a crossroads, awaiting its future amidst the pervading wave of privatization and commercialization. It is hoped that this huge institution will continue to survive—in one form or another—amid what appears to be a tumultuous time ahead.

Viability of the current vernacularization initiative in some regions could be constrained should institutions like EMPDA go fully private or commercial before an appropriate mechanism that could cater to their needs is put into place. Should the government decide to let go of EMPDA without a carefully designed alternative, some regions may face serious difficulties. It should be emphasized that the very policy that claims to promote them should not turn out to annihilate them.

Acknowledgments

This study was undertaken in Ethiopia in the summer of 1997. It was made possible through a grant from the Charles Leopold Mayer Foundation in France. I would like to express my indebtedness for the support extended to me by this foundation and its head, Mr. Michel Sauquet. I am also deeply indebted to my adviser, Prof. Philip Altbach, who has contributed immensely in making this study possible, for his constructive comments in the preparation of this chapter.

I also extend my appreciation to all government officials, private individuals, and scholars that participated in this study for their hospitality, time, and opinion. Last, but by no means least, I would like to extend my gratitude to Bezualem Meshesha and Workneh Endazenaw.

Notes

1. J. Dakin, B. Tiffen, and H.G. Widdowson, *Language in Education: The Problem in Commonwealth Africa and the Indo-Pakistan Subcontinent* (London: Oxford University Press, 1968); G. Waters, "Education and publishing in vernacular languages: Present state and future prospects in Papua New Guinea," *Asian/Pacific Book Development* 27, no. 3 (1997): 3–6; M. Takahashi, "Linguistic milieu and development of the national language of Indonesia," *Asian/Pacific Book Development* 27, no. 3 (1997): 7–8.

2. C.J. Daswani, "Mother tongue in primary school in India," *Asian/Pacific Book Development* 27, no. 3 (1997): 9–10.

3. Internet: http://www.pbs.org (PBS, 1997)

4. T. Bloor and W. Tamrat, "Multilingualism and Education: The Case of Ethiopia," in *Language and Education* (British Studies in Applied Linguistics, 11), eds. G.M. Blue and R. Mitchell (British Association for Applied Linguistics, 1996): 52–59.

5. M.A. Mazrui and A.M. Mazrui, *The Power of Babel: Language and Governance in the African Experience* (Chicago: University of Chicago Press, 1998).

6. Ibid., 71.

7. A. Bamgbose, "Introduction: The Changing Role of the Mother Tongue in Education," in *Mother Tongue Education: The West African Experience*, ed. A. Bamgbose (Paris: UNESCO, 1976): 9–26.

8. T. Awoniyi, "Mother Tongue Education in West Africa: A Historical Background," in *Mother Tongue Education: The West African Experience*, ed. A. Bamgbose (Paris: UNESCO, 1976): 27–42.

9. Bamgbose, "Introduction: The Changing Role," 9.

10. Ibid., 9–10.

11. M.A. Mazrui and A.M. Mazrui, *The Power of Babel*, 71.

12. Dakin et al. *Language in Education*, 20.

13. Ibid., 21.

14. In C. Okonkwo, *Language in African Education: A Comparative Analysis of the Curricular Elements of School Texts* (Occasional Papers Series) (Buffalo: Comparative Education Center, State University of New York at Buffalo, 1979), 2.

15. M.K. Gandhi, quoted in C. Okonkwo, op cit.: 3.

16. R. Tagore, quoted, in C. Okonkwo, op cit.: 4.

17. UNESCO (1953), B.J. Caroll (1961), P. Wingard (1963), and Nigeria Educational Research Council (1971) all quoted in C. Okonkwo, op cit.: 4.

18. M. Woodhall, "Cost-effectiveness of Publishing Educational Materials in African Languages," in *ADEA Working Group on Books and Learn-*

ing Materials, ed. Maureen Woodhall (London: ADEA, 1997): 1–24.

19. T. Bloor and W. Tamrat, "Multilingualism and Education," 57.

20. P.G. Altbach, "Servitude of the Mind? Education, Dependency, and Neocolonialism," in *Comparative Education*, ed. P.G. Altbach, et al. (NY: Macmillan, 1982): 469–484.

21. ADEA, "Language Policy and Planning in Senegal," *ADEA Newsletter* 8, no 4 (1996): 8–10.

22. Henry Chakava, quoted in K. Komarek, "Publishing in Africa or African Publishing?" *African Publishing Review* 6, no. 6 (1997): 1–2.

23. B.N. Peirce and S.G. Ridge, "Multilingualism in Southern Africa," *Annual Review of Applied Linguistics* 17 (1997): 170–190.

24. Ibid., 181.

25. T. Wagaw, *Education in Ethiopia: Prospect and Retrospect* (Ann Arbor: University of Michigan Press, 1979).

26. Bender, in M.A. Mazrui and A.M. Mazrui, *The Power of Babel*, 6.

27. T. Wagaw, *Education in Ethiopia*.

28. Ibid.

29. T. Negash, *Rethinking Education in Ethiopia* (Uppsala, Sweden: Nordiska Afrika Institutet, 1996).

30. Ibid., 82.

31. In 1995–96, there were 3,380,068 students in 9,704 primary schools, 407,851 students in 1,304 junior secondary schools, and 402,753 students in 346 senior secondary schools. During this time, the SNNPR, Oromiya, Tigray, and Amhara regions built 122, 116, 85, and 64 primary schools respectively. The total percentage increase of schools from 1994–95 to 1995–96 was an amazing 4.6, on average varying within regions.

32. H. Marcus, *A History of Ethiopia* (Los Angeles: University of California Press, 1994).

33. T. Teferra, "A Sociolinguistic Survey of Language Use and Attitudes Towards Language in Ethiopia: Implications for Language Policy in Education," (Doctoral dissertation) (Washington: Graduate School of Georgetown University, 1977).

34. A. Wassie, "Privatization and the Challenges for Publishing in Ethiopia," in *The Challenge of the Market: Privatization and Publishing in Africa*, ed. P.G. Altbach (Chestnut Hill, MA: Research and Information Center, Bellagio Publishing Network, 1996): 47–61.

35. T. Wagaw, *The Development of Higher Education and Social Science: An Ethiopian Experience* (East Lansing: Michigan State University Press, 1990).

36. M. Woodhall, "Cost-effectiveness," 12.

37. Eastman, in T. Bloor and W. Tamrat, "Multilingualism and Education."
38. M. Woodhall, "Cost-effectiveness," 5.
39. C.J. Daswani, "Mother tongue," 9.
40. ADEA, "Language Policy and Planning in Senegal."
41. G. Waters, "Education and Publishing in Vernacular Languages: Present State and Future Prospects in Papua New Guinea," *Asian/Pacific Book Development* 27, no. 3 (1997): 3–6.
42. ADEA, "Language Policy and Planning in Senegal," 9.
43. M. Sow, "Publishing in National Languages: Some Key Issues in Guinea," *African Publishing Review* 6, no. 6 (1998): 4–5.
44. T. Bloor and W. Tamrat, "Multilingualism and Education."
45. C.J. Daswani, "Mother Tongue."
46. B.N. Peirce and S.G. Ridge, "Multilingualism in Southern Africa," 173.
47. Tekeste Negash, *Rethinking Education in Ethiopia.*
48. *Addis Tribune* (1998). "Prime Minister Meles Speaks with *Financial Times.*" Internet: http://AddisTribune.EthiopiaOnline.Net/Archives/1998/03/06-03-98/Meles-83.htm
49. T. Wagaw, *The Development of Higher Education*, 53.
50. A. Wassie, "Privatization and the Challenges for Publishing," 50–51.
51. About seven Swedish kroner is equivalent to 1 U.S. dollar.
52. T. Negash, *Rethinking Education in Ethiopia*, 59.
53. M. Terefe, *Distribution of Instructional Materials in Ethiopia* (in Amharic) (Addis Ababa: EMPDA, July 1997).
54. Educational Materials Production and Distribution Agency, *Book and Price List for 1996–1997 Academic Year* (Addis Ababa: EMPDA, September 1997).
55. C. McNab, *Language Policy and Language Practice: Implementation Dilemmas in Ethiopian Education* (Stockholm: Institute of International Education, University of Stockholm, 1986).
56. Ministry of Education, *Formative Evaluation of the Try Out Project of the New Curriculum Materials of Grades 2 and 6—FENC2/6: Summary Report* (Addis Ababa: Curriculum Evaluation and Educational Research Coordination, Institute for Curriculum Development and Research, August 1996).
57. The minimum monthly wage of a government employee is 105 birr. Seven birr is equivalent to 1 U.S. dollar.
58. T. Wagaw, *The Development of Higher Education*, 24.

6

Publishing in Local Languages in Nigeria: A Publisher's Perspective

Victor U. Nwankwo

Introduction

Nigeria is a country of 102 million people, with about 250 nationalities and as many distinct indigenous languages.[1] The size of language groups varies from as much as 21 million for major languages (Hausa), to only a few hundreds for some minor ones. Nigeria became independent from British colonial rule in 1960. Politically it is structured as a federation, which was thought suitable for such a vast country of plural ethnicity. There are 36 states, each with its own executive, legislature, and judiciary. The states are further divided into administrative units—local government areas that now number 774. Table 1 lists Nigeria's 36 states (and Abuja), with population size and major (and minor) languages spoken.

The military has run the national affairs of Nigeria as a unitary system for 28 of its 38 post-independence years. This has distorted Nigeria's federalism, undermined the development of democratic institutions, institutionalized corruption, and generally impoverished the people. As the country transitions to democratic governance in May 1999, a "power shift" from the North to the South, rather than good governance, has become a distracting political issue. Because the national question is necessarily linked with national language development, this conflict has affected the implementation of the national language policy.

It is now conventional wisdom that the mother tongue or the language of the immediate community is the best medium of instruction for effective literacy. Thought is materialized through language. Learning is impaired when the form of linguistic and cognitive competence required in school is at variance with what is practiced and valued at home. Most West African countries have, in recognition of this, proposed the use of the local language during a child's early years of schooling. A report produced by the Working Group on Educational Research and Policy Analysis

Table 1
Population by States with Language Groups

State	Population (1996)	Major Language(s) spoken (or language groups)
1. Abia (includes part of Ebonyi)	2,663,136	Igbo
2. Adamawa	2,366,389	Chamba, Fulfude, Higgi, Kilba, *Minor languages:* Babur, Bachama, Bata, Baya, Bile, Bura, Bwatye, Cogla, Fali, Gira Matakam, Gombi, Gude, Hausa, Hona, Jibu, Jirai, Kanuri, Kauakuru, Koma, Lamja, Lunguda Lala, Marghi, Mbula, Mudang, Musanye, Nganda, Njaye, Sukur, Tur, Vemgo, Vomi, Vere Yungur, Waga, Wakari Jukun, Wula, Yandung
3. Akwa Ibom	2,746,743	Ibibio, Obolo
4. Anambra	3,227,830	Igbo
5. Bauchi (includes Gombe)	5,022,146	Fulfude / Hausa *Minor languages:* Angas, Bolewa, Chamo, Gubi, Jarawa, Jeawa, Junkun, Kare-Kare, Kirfawa, Kobiwa, Kudawa, Mbutawa, Miyawa, Ngamo, Ningawa, Sayawa, Shirawa, Terawa, Warijawa, Zaranda, Zulawa
6. Bayelsa	incl. in Rivers	Igbo, Izon, Kolokuma, Nembe
7. Benue	3,099,276	Idoma (including Agatu and Igede), Tiv *Minor languages:* Afor, Basange, Igala, Jukuns
8. Borno	2,927,178	Kanuri, Shuwa *Minor languages:* Babur, Bade, Buduma, Bura, Chibok, Dhwede, Fulfude, Gamergu, Hausa, Kalembu, Mandara, Manga, Marghi, Mobbar, Ngamo, Ngizin, Ngoshe
9. Cross River	2,206,114	Efik, Ejagham, Igede, Lokaa, Mbembe
10. Delta	2,952,928	Igbo, Isoko, Itsekiri, Izon, Urhobo

Table 1 (continued)

11. Ebonyi	incl. in Enugu and Abia	Igbo
12. Edo	2,475,893	Edo, Esan, Etsako
13. Ekiti	incl. in Ondo	Yoruba
14. Enugu (includes part of Ebonyi)	3,641,121	Igbo
15. Gombe	incl. in Bauchi	Bolewa, Dadiya, Fulani, Hausa, Jukun, Tangale, Tarawa, Tula, Waja
16. Imo	2,798,206	Igbo
17. Jigawa	3,237,123	Fulani, Hausa, Kanuri, Mangawa, Teshina, Warjawa
18. Kaduna	4,599,824	Bassa, Chamai, Gbagyi/Gwari, Hausa, Ikulu Jaba, Kadara, Kagoma, Kagoro, Kaje, Kajuru, Kamuku, Karo, Kataf, Konin Kon, Koro, Kurama, Mada, Morwa, Ninzom, Rumada, Yaskuna, Zango
19. Kano	6,876,507	Hausa (incl. Maguzawa)
20. Katsina	4,225,091	Hausa
21. Kebbi	2,328,604	Borgawa, Dakarkari, Dandawa, Hausa, Jarmawa, Kabawa, Kambari, Kengawa, Zabarmawa
22. Kogi	2,417,836	Basange, Ebira, Haysa, Igala, Kakanda, Nupe, Ogori, Yoruba
23. Kwara	1,765,053	Baruba, Bassa, Fulfude, Hausa, Ijumu, Kambari, Nupe, Oworo, Yoruba
24. Lagos	6,947,019	Yoruba
25. Nasarawa	incl. in Plateau	Afor, Arago, Fulfude, Ganawuri, Gode, Kanem, Kanuri, Nupe, Yagwamama
26. Niger	2,795,108	Bassa, Bassange, Bussa Dakarkari, Gade, Gbagyi/Gwari, Gwandara, Hausa, Kakanda, Kambari, Kamuku, Koro, Kyama, Ngwai, Nupe, Pongu, Tarok
27. Ogun	2,660,240	Yoruba
28. Ondo (includes Ekiti)	4,261,558	Yoruba

Table 1 (continued)

29. Osun	2,460,090	Yoruba
30. Oyo	3,985,297	Yoruba
31. Plateau (includes Nasarawa)	3,823,348	Basange, Beron, Gbagyi/Gwari, Jarawa, Magavul, Miyango, Ngas, Rukuba, Tarok
32. Rivers (includes Bayelsa)	5,100,227	Ahoada, Igbo, Ijo, Ikwere, Kalabari, Obolo, Ogba, Ogoni
33. Sokoto (includes Zamfara)	5,159,697	Achipawa, Dakarkari, Dukawa, Hausa, Jarmawa, Kambari, Kamuku, Shangawa, Zabarmawa
34. Taraba	1,723,732	Bali, Baya, Bwatye, Chamba, Daka, Dnoro, Fulfude, Kakara, Kentoh Mambila, Kona Jonjo, Kunini, Kurkun, Kuteb, Mbum, Mummuye, Panso, Tigon, Tiv, Wakari/Jukun
35. Yobe	1,575,699	Bade, Bolewa, Hausa, Kanuri, Karekare, Mangawa, Mobbar, Ngizim, Terawa
36. Zamfara	incl. in Sokoto	Hausa, Kambari
37. Abuja (Federal Capital Territory)	445,399	Cosmopolitan, Ebira, Gbagyi/Gwari, Nupe
TOTAL	102,514,412	

Note: This table was compiled by the author from various sources, including Onigu Otite, *Ethnic Pluralism and Ethnicity in Nigeria* (Ibadan, Nigeria: Shaneson C. I., 1990), and personal communication.

(WGER&PA) of the Association for the Development of Education in Africa (ADEA) on language acquisition and learning outcomes, based on a study in six African countries, including Nigeria, concluded:

> With regard to pedagogical effectiveness, research shows that language of learning (LOL) policies which favour mother tongues in the early years of basic education result in improved and faster acquisition of knowledge by pupils. Furthermore mother tongue LOL instruction is effective in promoting the acquisition of second language competencies.[2]

Specifically, research findings in the three major languages in Nigeria support the mother tongue medium policy, as well:

> While Ala (1983), Ande (1990) and Akinbote (1995) found that children taught different subjects in Yoruba performed significantly better than their counterparts taught in English, Okonkwo (1979) and Umaru (1983) also found Igbo and Hausa respectively as more facultative to learning than English among school children.[3]

This chapter will examine the status of the implementation of Nigeria's national language policy; discuss its effects on publishing in indigenous languages in Nigeria as an essential and sustainable activity for the achievement of permanent literacy; and proffer suggestions for moving its implementation forward.

National Language Policy

Nigerian pupils in primary and secondary schools reflect a wide range of linguistic backgrounds. Generally, children from smaller language groups have to speak, as their second or third languages, the dominant languages in their regions. The result is that some Nigerians speak three or four indigenous languages. The language of instruction in primary schools is generally the language of the immediate community, except in private schools or in public schools in high-income urban areas. The "language of the immediate community" is not the mother tongue for some pupils. In all primary schools, written work is in English; it is in an indigenous language only when it is taught as a subject. At the secondary school level, the language of instruction is English. English is also the language in which examinations are written. In both primary and secondary schools, the textbooks are still in English. In the colonial days, "vernacular" was banned from being spoken on the school premises. In effect, for those in the boarding school, the indigenous language might not be spoken for the 12 weeks of the school term. All that has changed now.

The National Policy on Education (NPE), which was first promulgated in 1977, provided for the use of the mother tongue or the language of the immediate community as a medium of instruction in early formal education. It specified that English should be taught by specialist English teachers and that each pupil must, in addition to English and to his/her own language, learn one of the three major languages of Nigeria—Hausa, Igbo, or Yoruba. The NPE was revised in 1981. The objective of the first language program was that at the end of junior secondary school students should be able to express themselves correctly in the prescribed Nigerian language, including the use of the appropriate lexicon and figures of speech; discuss elements of the oral tradition of the language with familiarity; read and appreciate literature; carry out continuous writing in the Nigerian language, employing correct grammar, punctuation etc.; and generally acquire the skill to pursue further studies in the Nigerian language.

In Table 2, Omamor has captured the essential details of the policy objectives of the language policy, as well as the strategies for achieving them.[4]

Table 2
Details of the Nigerian Language Policy

Level	Provision
Pre-primary Education	• Medium of instruction will be principally the mother tongue or the language of the immediate community. • The orthography for many languages will be developed. • Textbooks will be produced for these languages.
Primary Education	• The government will see to it that the medium of instruction in the first three years of primary school is the mother tongue of the language of the immediate community; English will be used at a later stage.
Secondary Education	• Students should study the language of their own area in addition to one of the three major languages, subject to the availability of teachers. • The core curriculum, i.e. the group of subjects that every pupil must study in addition to his/her specialties, must include one Nigerian language. • French is an elective. • Development and projection of Nigerian culture, art, language, etc.
Tertiary Education	• The awarding of degrees will be conditional on the passing of a compulsory first-year course on the social organization, customs, culture, and history of our diverse peoples.

Implementation

In the 18 years since the revised national education and language policy was published, significant work has been done.

OFFICIAL USAGE

Nigerian languages have been recognized as official languages for conducting legislative debates. The relevant sections of the 1995 draft Constitution provide that the business of the national and state legislative houses shall be conducted in English and that Nigerian languages shall become additional languages of business of the House as may be determined by the respective national or state assemblies.[5]

The indigenous language content of radio and television broadcasts across the country has increased. Major international radio stations, such as the British Broadcasting Corporation (BBC) and the Voice of America (VOA), air Hausa and other language programs.

DICTIONARIES, PRIMERS, AND DESCRIPTIVE GRAMMARS

The Nigerian Educational Research and Development Council (NERDC)[6] has produced a series of glossaries of science and mathematical terms in the nine major Nigerian languages.[7] It has developed dictionaries of legislative terms in the three main Nigerian languages. It has also developed primers, general dictionaries, and descriptive grammars for the three major languages.

STANDARD ORTHOGRAPHIES

The missionaries who published first religious material and then educational books and newsletters began orthographic and publishing development in Nigeria's indigenous languages. Now the NERDC has developed standard orthography for 36 Nigerian languages. Table 3 lists the languages and the states where they are spoken.

CURRICULUM GUIDELINES

The NERDC has prepared curriculum guidelines that are in wide circulation for teaching Igbo, Hausa, and Yoruba as first languages. Curriculum guidelines for teaching these languages as a second language have been developed. Some states have developed standard guidelines for dominant languages in their respective states.

The NERDC carried out the critique of the Agricultural Science Primary Curriculum, which was translated in-house into Hausa, Igbo, and

Table 3
Orthography of Nigerian Languages

No.	Language	States Where the Language is Spoken
1	Hausa	Bauchi, Gombe, Jigawa, Kano, Katsina, Kebbi, Niger, Sokoto, Zamfara
2	Igbo	Abia, Anambra, Bayelsa, Delta, Ebonyi, Enugu, Imo
3	Yoruba	Ekiti, Kogi, Kwara, Lagos, Ogun, Ondo, Osun, Oyo
4	Efik	Cross River
5	Edo	Edo
6	Tiv	Benue
7	Fulfude	Adamawa, Taraba
8	Kanuri	Borno, Yobe
9	Ijo	Rivers
10	Ibibio	Akwa Ibom
11	Nupe	Kogi, Kwara, Niger
12	Beron	Plateau
13	Idoma	Benue
14	Kalabari	Rivers
15	Ebira	Abuja (Federal Capital Territory), Kogi
16	Igala	Benue, Kogi
17	Isoko	Delta
18	Kaje	Kaduna
19	Gbagyi/Gwari	FCT, Kaduna, Niger, Plateau
20	Bwatye	Adamawa, Taraba
21	Esan	Edo
22	Bura	Adamawa, Borno
23	Ikwere	Rivers
24	Urhobo	Delta
25	Wakari Jukun	Adamawa, Taraba
26	Obolo	Akwa Ibom, Rivers
27	Igede	Benue, Cross River
28	Mbembe	Cross River
29	Tarok	Plateau
30	Lokaa	Cross River
31	Ejagham	Cross River
32	Etsako	Edo
33	Koro	Kaduna
34	Marghi	Adamawa, Borno
35	Mumuye	Adamawa, Taraba
36	Ngas	Plateau

Source: Language Development Centre, NERDC.

Yoruba languages. It has also produced teaching curricula for junior secondary school and senior secondary school levels in the Efik language. Some states have developed standard guidelines for dominant languages in their respective states.

TRANSLATION

Work has started in the translation of core subjects into the national languages. Textbooks in Integrated Science and Handicraft Education have been translated into the three major languages of Hausa, Igbo, and Yoruba.

INSTITUTIONAL DEVELOPMENT

A National Language Institute has been established at Aba, Abia State, for training teachers in Nigerian languages.

Some pilot projects provide valuable experience in the provision of books in indigenous languages. The Ife Six-Year Primary Project for a major Nigerian language and the Rivers Readers' Project for a number of relatively small languages are some examples.

The University of Ibadan started teaching Hausa, Igbo, and Yoruba in 1962. The establishment of a Department of Linguistics and Nigerian Languages in 1962 made possible the launching of degree-level training in this field. Other universities in the country, and indeed in Europe and North America, now have degree programs—some up to doctoral level—in the three major languages.

Customary and *sharia* courts are conducted in the language of the locality. Magistrates and superior courts are conducted in English. All official documentation, including government gazettes, laws, and court and legislative records are, however, still in English.

Take-off Needs and Constraints

Obviously, substantial work has been done. But the national language program has not taken off; nor is there any discernible take-off schedule or plan. The attempts made to identify the problems militating against this are described below.

AVAILABILITY OF TRAINED TEACHERS

Recent statistical figures show that Nigeria has a total of 14,796,074 primary school pupils, 419,997 teaching staff, 40,204 schools, 405,002 classes, and 69,730 nonteaching staff.[8] This gives an average teacher/pupil ratio of 1:29—which is even better than the National Policy on Education target of 1:30 "for the near future." Average primary school attendance is an impressive 90 percent.

Pupils moving from primary level 3 to 4 have to be weaned from their respective local languages to English as a medium of instruction and learning. The Tanzanian experience, for example, has shown that learning is impaired when pupils do not acquire adequate proficiency in English at the time of change to English as the medium of instruction.[9] As the NPE envisages, for a seamless transition, specialist English teachers should teach English during the three years of primary education when instruction is in the local languages.

For the program to take off and maintain the same level of attendance and the same ratio of teachers to pupils, teachers need therefore to:

- teach six core subjects in national languages to Year 1 primary pupils;
- teach English to primary school pupils in preparation for transition to English as the medium of instruction after Year 3; and
- teach one of the three major languages as a second language to Year 1 junior secondary students.

Specialist teachers in languages need to be trained with special emphasis on the methodology that is best suited to teaching in those languages. They also need to be knowledgeable in the medium their respective mother tongue and in teaching materials in that particular mother tongue. Nothing short of a carefully planned and funded program of massive production of specialist teachers can lead to the realization of the objectives of national language education.

There has been no visible increase in the enrollments of relevant language departments, the likely candidates for specialist training in English and the national languages. Nor has the National Language Institute—established to train the many teachers needed for the take off and sustenance of the language policy—lived up to that task, perhaps for lack of funding. It has established a secondary school instead!

EXAMINATION PROGRAMS

As Brann has rightly pointed out, teaching a language is not the same as teaching *in* a language. And the "methods of teaching a second language (L2) are quite different from the methods of teaching a first language (L1), i.e. separate papers would have to be developed for Hausa, Igbo and Yoruba as L1 and L2."[10]

Examination programs provide the means to test students' learning achievements. They reveal, therefore, the level of the national government's recognition of, and plan for, what is being taught. The Cambridge Local

Table 4
Entries for O-level Public Examination WAEC Received in 1985

Language	Entries for O-level in 1985 (thousands)	Remarks
English	550	
Yoruba	100	Adequate
Igbo	50	Modest
Hausa	30	Inadequate
French	3	
Efik	2	Modest in proportion to population number
Arabic	1	

Source: Brann, 1999.

Note: 1985 was a bumper year for WAEC.

Examinations Syndicate introduced Efik, Hausa, Igbo, and Yoruba to the O-level examinations program 50 years ago. Since then, no other Nigerian language has been added to the O-level examination program, not even by the West African Examinations Council (WAEC), which was established in 1952 to control certification for primary and postprimary education. Table 4 presents entries received by WAEC for the 1985 O-level public examinations in Arabic, Efik, English, French, Igbo, Hausa, and Yoruba.[11] There is obviously an acute shortage of secondary school graduates trained in national languages, except Yoruba, from which the teachers for primary schools will be recruited.

While the number of entries for English has not changed (550,000 in 1985, against 524,000 in 1995), performance has deteriorated. Of the 524,290 pupils entered for English language in 1995, 290,237 (55 percent) failed outright. Does this failure rate reflect poor acquisition of communication skills in English among pupils? Current thinking is beginning to seek the answer to this question in the design of the examination paper itself.

To enable a far larger number of pupils to pass the English O-level examination, Brann has suggested that the English paper should be updated in standard Nigerian English (SNE), in accord with educational research from the past 25 years. This entails a decision on acceptable Nigerian standards of pronunciation, morpho-syntax, lexicon, idiom, and style, which may be quite distinct from the British standard. Brann further observes indications that Nigerian English has come to standardize forms that are now acceptable nationally and which should, therefore, form part of the curriculum. In any case, it is important to resolve the problem of failures of English papers before the take off of the language policy.

What can be done to lighten the burden of introducing local languages as media of instruction in schools in a country with more than 250 national languages? To enhance the teaching of Nigerian languages at the secondary level, the pool from which ultimately teachers for primary schools will be recruited, Brann has made an innovative proposal that the "network" languages of Edo, Efik/Ibibio, Fula, Ijo, Igala, Idoma, Nupe, Kanuri, and Tiv be taught to an O-level, with corresponding examinations by the West African Examinations Council. The subject/paper should not be limited to only one standard form of the language. Instead, the culture and literature of the whole group should be taught, while the language forms of one or several standards are considered for the examination syllabus. For the others, all Nigerian "network languages" would be taught in their ethno-linguistic groups as the mother tongue or first language (L1), with a choice of standards. For example, the main standard for Edo language is Bini. While the literature of the whole Edoid (network) group is taught, pupils from other languages in the group, such as Esan, Etsako, Isoko and Urhobo, should have a choice to be examined based on standards of their respective languages. One cannot agree more that "this is an innovative approach to language education, starting with the group and then going to the particular identificational member speech form."[12]

POLITICAL FACTORS

Political sensitivities cause resistance to policies perceived to offend certain groups. More than half of Nigeria's 36 states are either monoethnic (and monolingual) or, where bilingual, have one or two dominant language groups. In such cases, the choice of the language of immediate environment is easily resolved in favor of the dominant language(s). In some states, however, a totally different language is spoken every few kilometers. In such cases, the choice of language of immediate locality becomes a political issue. The decision to use one language as the medium of instruction can be interpreted as "denial of rights," "institutionalising deprivation," and "magnifying long standing discrepancies between 'major' and 'minor' language groups."[13] The National Primary Commission is responsible for the development of primary education in Nigeria. It has supervisory control over 37 State Primary Education Boards (SPEB) and 774 Local Government Primary Education Committees. With the unity structure imposed by army rule, even those states that had no problems choosing the language of the immediate environment have been affected by lack of progress in others.

In most cities and urban areas, even in monolingual states, there would technically be no problem as to what constitutes the language of the immediate environment. In very large urban centers, such as Lagos and the federal capital territory of Abuja, *non-indigenes* may well outnumber *indigenes*. However, in many such urban areas, the language of the *indigenes* is often the language of street commerce, political rallies, and verbal communication in workplaces. It is not difficult to agree with Anyanwu's suggestion that in such cases the medium of instruction should be the language of the *indigenes*, as this is effectively the language of the immediate environment. Indeed, studies elsewhere have shown that children whose language of instruction *from the very beginning* is a foreign language—different from the home language—do not suffer from any language drawbacks.[14] This point becomes significant when proposals for book provision are discussed.

NATIONAL LANGUAGE BOOK NEEDS

A survey by Fajemisin[15] on books in indigenous languages published in Nigeria reveals that of more than 10,000 titles published in 1990–94, only 989 (9.9 percent) were in indigenous languages. This is, however, 50 percent more than 604 titles published in the 10 years prior to the period of study (1981–90). The indigenous languages found to be widely published were Edo, Efik, Hausa, Ibibio, Igala, Igbo, Tiv, Urhobo, and Yoruba. Not surprisingly, the three major indigenous languages accounted for 91 percent (900 titles out of 989) for 1990–94 and 93 percent (562 titles out of 604) for 1980–90.

Fajemisin's survey gives a clear lead to materials for children in indigenous languages—429 titles (43.4 percent) of the total of 989 published between 1990 and 1994. A closer look shows that these are general readers and grammar books for the major languages. However, there are at least three separate titles on the core primary subjects in the three main languages of Hausa, Igbo, and Yoruba. There were also single titles in other languages, such as Efik, Gbagyi/Gwari, and Ibibio. The distribution of pupils across school age for 1995 is given in Table 5. Table 6 provides estimates of Nigeria's national language book needs for launching the national language policy in primary and junior secondary schools and for every subsequent year.

Table 7 shows the three major language groups—Hausa, Igbo, and Yoruba—constituting 58 percent of the total population, while the 12 larg-

Table 5
The Distribution of Population of School Age (1995)

	Primary 6–11 yr. (millions)	Jr. Secondary 12–14 yr. (millions)	Sr. Secondary 15–17 yr. (millions)	Tertiary 18–25 yr. (millions)
Male	8.3	3.6	3.4	7.1
Female	8.1	3.5	3.2	7.3
Total	16.4	7.1	6.6	14.4

Note: Projected from 1991 National Population Census.

Table 6
Estimates of Books Needed for Implementing National Language Policy

Level	Details	Books Needed (thousands)
Primary 1 only	*Student's text:* for a population of approximately 3 million pupils, 4 core subjects, 1 pupil to a pair of textbook and workbook (3 m x 4 x 2)	24,000
Primary 1-3	*Teacher's text:* 1 guide book per teacher at pupil-teacher ratio of 30:1	100
Junior Secondary	Pupils are required to study one of the three major languages of Hausa, Igbo, or Yoruba, not as mother tongues but as a second language. It is feasible to start the program in all the junior secondary classes at once.	4,700

Note: There were a total of 14.8 million school age children at the primary level (1-6). See Saxone Akhaine, "Nurturing Education." There were 3.24 million school age children at the secondary level (1-6). *PC Globe* (Tempe, AZ: 1992).

est language groups account for 86 percent. A staged implementation of the national language program starting with the three major languages and then the next top nine would be a good take off point because it would involve a significant proportion of the population. involve a significant proportion of the population.

Publishing Issues

Publishing in Nigeria is essentially a private enterprise activity. The distinguishing feature of textbook provision in Nigeria—as against the practice in most African countries—is that authorship, production, and distribution are normally private initiatives; and, except for occasional government or World Bank book intervention schemes, book provision to pupils is by parental purchase. The initiative for commissioning works and publishing them originates from publishers; naturally, this is an investment decision. Nigerian publishers have not failed to show readiness to invest in primary school textbooks in indigenous languages.

As stated earlier, in anticipation of the implementation of the language policy, Nigerian publishers have developed textbooks on core subjects in local languages. The defining act of publishing is necessarily a business decision, which is in dynamic tension with a publisher's sense of calling in what is essentially a culture industry. In terms of economics, the parameters for publishing in local languages are generally uncharted. Data for informed projections are dependent on assessments of the likely consequences of government programs. Economic disaster awaits a publisher whose projections are frustrated by the government's failure to follow

Table 7
Disposition of Language and Ethnic Groups
(percent of population)

Languages	%	Ethnic Groups	%
Hausa	21	Hausa	21
Yoruba	20	Yoruba	21
Igbo	17	Igbo	18
Fulfude	9	Fulani	11
Ibibio-Efik	5	Ibibio	7
Kanuri	4	Kanuri	4
Tiv	3	Edo	3
Izon	2	Tiv	2
Edo	2	Izon	2
Nupe	1	Byra	2
Igala	1	Nupe	1
Idoma	1		
Subtotal	86	Subtotal	92
Other	14	Other	8

Source: *PC Globe* (Tempe, AZ: 1992).

through on its programs. Several Nigerian publishers have produced books in the core primary level subjects. All these books have been lying in their warehouses unsold. Though investment returns were projected for no more than three years, there have been no returns on the investments of the publishers for developing and producing these titles after nine years! As there is no known program of the government to implement the language policy, the fate of this investment still looks bleak.

The greatest cost of publishers in Nigeria is expended on translation, as many materials already exist in English. To translate into local languages, translators are demanding high—but perhaps fair—rates per page, particularly for science texts. This has to do with timing and, of course, supply and demand of technically competent translators. There is also the cost of lithography and, finally, marketing.

At the Association for the Development of Education in Africa (ADEA) Working Group on Books and Learning Materials Seminar on Book Policy in National Languages held in Dakar, Senegal in October 1997, it was recognized that for publications in indigenous languages to be sustainable, they should be integrated into the general framework of book supply to schools and subjected to the same procedures of conception, editing, production, printing, and distribution as materials in English, French, or Portuguese.[16] This is impossible unless the program takes off. And publishers are in a dilemma whether to start developing their publications now for a market with no guaranteed future.

The attitude of the Nigerian federal government is like shooting oneself in the foot. Fourth Dimension's dictionary of primary science, which was developed by the NERDC, a federal agency, in fulfilment of its role in the language policy, was not selected for procurement in the first and now the second World Bank primary school textbook procurement project.[17] Neither was it selected in the current Petroleum Trust Fund (PTF) textbook procurement project. Yet, as of now, it is the only reference tool for the translation of primary science and mathematics textbooks into the top nine Nigerian languages, spoken by more than 80 percent of the Nigerian people. The only logical conclusion is that the government has no intention, now or in the near future, of implementing the National Policy on Education as it relates to the national language policy.

Conclusion

It is typical that the failure so far of this policy is due not to poor formulation but to poor policy implementation. According to management specialist, Peter Drucker, the best way to predict the future is to create it.

What is required at this stage is a well thought out and integrated implementation program that links language planning to economic planning.

The Introduction to the National Policy on Education concludes:

> Government has therefore set up a National Education Policy Implementation Committee which translated the Policy into a workable blueprint that will guide the bodies whose duty it is to implement educational policy, and will also develop a monitoring system of the progress of the planned educational evolution to ensure that infrastructures are prepared and bottlenecks removed in time to facilitate the effective [and] smooth implementation of this policy on Education.[18]

The document mentions several bodies that have been assigned implementation responsibilities without coordination. A coordination agency should be created with representation from all stakeholders, clear achievement benchmarks, and a defined transition timetable.

As part of its program, this agency should, among other things, set out to determine how many languages exist in Nigeria. Omamor has made a practical recommendation: students of linguistics should, as a graduation requirement, undertake the description of some aspects, such as phonology and grammar, of either languages that have not previously been the subject of any academic study or an unexplored area of some of the better known languages.[19]

To facilitate investment by publishers in developing new books in indigenous languages, the government should set up a machinery to provide translation and development support. The NERDC should be strengthened to play a key role here.

The government should seriously consider and, where necessary, adopt innovative proposals to improve the standard of English at school. Finally, the National Language Institute should be strengthened to play its role in the training of language teachers.

Notes

1. Projected from 1991 National Population Census.

2. M. Woodhall, "Cost-effectiveness of Publishing Educational Materials in African Languages," in *ADEA Working Group on Books and Learning Materials*, ed. Maureen Woodhall (London: ADEA, 1997).

3. Olusegun Akinbote, "Effects of Language of instruction on some Nigeria primary school pupils' achievement in social studies," *Studies in Education*, 2 no 1 (1995).

4. A.P. Omamor, "Linguistics and the 1977/1981 National Language Policy Education in Nigeria," *The Language Studies: Journal of the National Institute for Nigerian Languages*, no 1 (December 1993): 44-53.

5. Federal Republic of Nigeria, *Report of the National Constitutional Conference 1994/95 (Draft Constitution 1995)* (Abuja: Fourth Dimension, 1995).

6. The NERDC was established in December 1998 with the merger of Nigeria Educational Research Council (NERC), Comparative Education Study and Adaptation Center (CESAC), Nigeria Book Development Council (NBDC), and the National Language Centre (NLC). NERDC serves as the think-tank on education. Its responsibilities pertinent to book publishing and development include formulating and implementing in a national policy on book development; undertaking and promoting book development and local authorship by ensuring the provision of adequate infrastructure facilities for book manufacture; encouraging the expansion of the local printing and publishing industry in order to facilitate book production; encouraging and promoting a reading culture through continual research into the needs of Nigerian readers; developing an effective book distribution sector to ensure a nationwide circulation; encouraging the establishment and strengthening of a professional association of the book industry in Nigeria; and serving as a center for the exchange of information on books and all related issues.

7. NERDC, 1987.

8. Saxone Akhaine, "Nurturing Education at the Roots," *The Guardian on Sunday* (Lagos: June 10, 1990).

9. Z.M. Roy-Campbell and M.A.S. Qorro, *The Language Crises in Tanzania* (Dar es Salaam: Mkuki Na Nyota Publishers, 1997).

10. Brann, "WAEC and Language Education," *The Guardian* (Lagos: 21 January 1999): 21.

11. Ibid.

12. Brann, "WAEC and Language Education."

13. A.P. Omamor, "Linguistics."

14. Ingrid Jung, "Towards Literate Societies: Publishing in Local Languages," in *Educational Publishing in Global Perspective*, ed. Shobhana Sosale (Washington: IBRD/The World Bank, 1999).

15. M.O. Fajemisin, *Current Perspectives in Indigenous Publishing in Nigeria* (Harare: African Publishers Network [APNET], 1994).

16. Carew Trefgarne. Unpublished report.

17. The World Bank provided a soft loan of US$120 million for the provision of textbooks in core subjects over the six years of primary school.

18. Federal Republic of Nigeria, 1981.

19. A.P. Omamor, "Linguistics."

7

Publishing in Indian Languages: Perspectives from the Subcontinent

Urvashi Butalia

Introduction

India is considered to be the third-largest publisher in English books in the world. Of the 19,000 to 22,000 titles published in the country annually, 40 to 50 percent are believed to be in English. And yet, India is a country with a rich and multilingual tradition. There are, at present, some 18 official languages—those that have been recognized by the state and are considered to have more than 1 million speakers each—and hundreds, even thousands, of dialects. Small, but dynamic, publishing traditions exist in several Indian languages. The following statistics provide a glimpse of the number of titles published in the different languages in India.

Although the picture provided by these statistics is correct in a broad sense, it is important to note at the outset that it is also open to question. Such statistics as there are on Indian publishing—and there are very few—are not particularly reliable. The most recent survey regarding the book industry was carried out in the early 1970s, with its results published in 1972.[1]

There is little doubt, however, that, despite the unreliability of the statistics, English is the main language of publishing, in terms of numbers as well as visibility. The question then is: how has English come to acquire such importance in India given its wealth of local languages? To understand this and the state of Indian language publishing, we need to look briefly at the history of English publishing in India.

English Publishing in India: An Historical Perspective

Any history of publishing in India needs to take printing as its starting point. Printing first came to India in the sixteenth century. Presses were set up around the southern coast and from there spread to other parts of the country following the missionaries who were the earliest printers/

Table 1
Titles Published by Language in India

Language	Number of Titles Published
English	9,922
Hindi	2,382
Tamil	1,319
Marathi	1,118
Bengali	1,104
Kannada	888
Gujarati	673
Malayalam	607
Telugu	540
Punjab	389
Oriya	245
Urdu	154
Assamese	148
Sanskrit	129
Others	51

Note: These figures are taken from the keynote address of Professor Indra Nath Choudhuri, "Problems of Book Publishing in Indian Languages," presented at the National Convention of Indian Language Publishers seminar held in 1993 in New Delhi. No date is given for the figures. The date of the seminar, however, suggests figures are from the early 1990s or the late 1980s.

publishers. The first books they produced were the Bible and other Christian works, published, by and large, in the Indian languages that were used to educate natives in the word of God.

The British came to be involved in publishing in India around the last quarter of the eighteenth century, mainly because they needed to ensure greater efficiency in their administrative system. The East India Company had changed in character from being a trading organization to a colonial state and its officers needed to interpret and process official documents that were in Indian languages. Suspicious of the reliability of native interpreters, they began to learn Indian languages and for this purpose developed primers and other books in these languages. At the same time, however, the expansion of the administrative infrastructure also meant that the British sought help from Indians who were speakers of English. Such people, it was felt, could communicate with the leaders and the masses, and also serve in administrative posts. Books in Indian languages and English therefore continued to be published until 1784, when the British government announced that henceforth those educated in English would be preferred for all posts in office. Immediately, knowledge of English became a mechanism for upward social mobility for Indians.

Nonetheless, books in Indian languages did not disappear completely. The establishment of Fort William College in 1800 created a demand for books in Indian languages, mostly to serve as textbooks. A year later, in 1801, William Carey founded the first of India's major printing establishments, the Serampore Mission Press. The Press, set up initially to publish translations of the Bible in Indian languages, went on to publish books in Bengali, Tamil, Telugu, Marathi, Oriya, and English for the college. It carried out work for the government, as well. Gradually, as other educational institutions were founded, publishing centers and printing presses were set up around them to service their educational needs. Slowly, however, the focus was shifting to English books.

In 1813, the Charter Act made education of the native population a state concern. As a result, a new and expanded educational system began to evolve and the textbook became the focus of the school curriculum. Now the need was greater than ever to ensure that the books being used were "reliable" and "trustworthy." But this was not a simple matter. It was clear that people could read better in their own languages than in English. A strategy was devised that could accommodate these seemingly contradictory requirements, whereby funds were made available for translations of English books into Indian languages. A number of textbook societies were subsequently set up; one of their tasks was to provide funds for the translation of English textbooks into Indian languages so that students could become familiar—albeit through their own languages—with English ideas and culture.

Over time, this strategy of colonizing the mind had the desired result. Familiarity with English culture also created a desire among many middle class Indians to read English books and to learn English. Libraries were set up in major towns and it became customary to spend money on books in English rather than Indian languages. The Calcutta Schoolbook Society, for example, published and sold more than 30,000 English books over the course of two years. At the India Office in London, Thomas Macaulay used this newfound interest in English to press for its recognition as the language of education and to suggest that more money be spent on English books than on any others.

Now that it was official policy to keep "unsuitable" books away from Indians, the British were able to more easily curb the number of books published in Indian languages. In 1847, they legislated a copyright law that made it compulsory for all books to be submitted for copyright verification. Indian publishers saw this as a move to control what was being published. Their suspicions were further strengthened when regular checks began to be kept on native presses and when reports were prepared on their output. Any transgression of boundaries could mean having one's license as a printer/publisher taken away. British concern about what was being printed in the Indian-language press could also result in government patronage being withdrawn. The Moostafee Press in Lucknow, one of the most important Urdu publishers, for example, was criticized for publishing "a lot of trash" and "sowing the seeds of wickedness and vice."

The Indigenous Publishing Scene

The historical account above focuses mainly on educational books. These made up the bulk of books published in India at the time. As in many developing countries, general or trade books were slow to develop in India. Until recently, about 80 percent of the book market was said to have been taken up by educational books; although recent years have brought some changes, the overall picture today remains much the same.

THE NATIONAL INITIATIVE

Although it was the missionaries who initiated publishing in the early days, it was individual Indians—who took upon themselves the task of making particular books available to readers—who carried this effort further and sustained it. In Tamil, for example, some of the earliest publishers were well known scholars and writers such as Anavarada Vinakayam Pillai, Thandavaraya Mudaliar, and U.V. Swaminathan Aiyar. They printed many of the Tamil classics and also set many precedents in terms of style and language. Interestingly, print runs of these early publications were based on prepublication subscriptions collected from prospective readers, and these were often considerable.

One of the first priorities of the Indian government after independence in 1948 was to develop educational books and materials that were "Indian" in character. As early as 1942, Indians in positions of power lobbied for a policy of nationalization of school textbooks immediately after independence. The idea was that books used for educational purposes in India should reflect a "national," rather than a colonial, approach. Changing textbooks, however, could not be done overnight; the program was devised in such a way that the change would be phased and gradual. In the interim, private sector publishers were free to tap this lucrative market. In the early stages, the state initiated various plans with which private sector publishers could be involved for publishing textbooks—sometimes handing out state contracts to them. Over the years, however, as the school textbook market was gradually taken over by the state, the share of the private sector declined. Today, school textbook publishing in India is largely in the hands of the public sector, although some niche areas still remain open for the private sector. These areas are largely related to English language textbooks.

Where general books were concerned, the situation was somewhat different. For many Indian languages, the 1920s to 1940s were important times. Nationalism was at its height and everywhere writers were coming together to create associations of progressive writers. These associations—in places as far apart as Uttar Pradesh, Andhra Pradesh, and Kerala—were set up by writers with socialist sympathies who ran reading groups and schools to encourage reading. Despite the checks and balances set up by the British, Indian language publishers were not afraid of publishing materials that might be considered controversial. It was in the 1930s that Ismat Chugtai, a well-known Urdu writer, published a story called "Lihaaf" ("The Quilt") which dealt with the taboo subject of women's sexuality. She was charged by the then British government with obscenity, but she won her case on the argument that if she was to be persecuted for writing about lesbianism—which the story deals with—then that implied that those persecuting her had knowledge of the subject and were therefore liable to prosecution themselves! All over the country, publishing in Indian languages remained dynamic and lively at this time.

These early decades of publishing in Indian languages were also interesting for other reasons. Nationalist sentiments were instrumental in building a close working relationship between authors and publishers; and this often enabled authors to play a leading role in the publication of their books. Because of the widespread involvement of literary figures in publishing in different languages, the early decades of the twentieth century also produced a number of translations, not only of foreign writers, but Indian writers from other Indian languages.

Gradually, however, this healthy state of affairs changed. Despite the widespread intention and commitment to developing publishing in Indian languages, in the years after independence, this did not happen. Partly this was because many of the promises of independence remained unfulfilled. Literacy rates, for example, were slow to improve, educational facilities remained inadequate, and overall government budgets allocated for these sectors were considerably reduced from past levels.

Overtime, the government's policy of nationalizing textbook production was to have a somewhat adverse effect on Indian language publishing.

Undercapitalized as most Indian language publishers are, the removal of this lucrative area of business meant that publishers were deprived of a dependable source of income and thus forced to look elsewhere. While some closed down their businesses, others, ever resourceful, turned this apparent disadvantage to their advantage and started to publish supplementary readers, "guidebooks," and "keys" to prescribed textbooks. These were books that would set out model questions and answers for exams and advise students on how to deal with particular subjects. Such was their success that in Maharashtra, in western India, a publisher of guidebooks called Navneet was even able to float a public limited company that did extremely well on the stock market. Other publishers turned to very specific areas marketing themselves as niche publishers.

Unlike the years before independence, when, all Indian languages were disparaged, the trajectories followed by Indian language publishing for different languages in the post-independence years were very different. With the partition of India into two countries, India and Pakistan, on the basis of religion, the Urdu language (written in the Arabic script)—until then the language of a large number of Indians from Punjab and the entire northern region—became identified as the language of Pakistan. In India, its place of importance was taken over by Hindi (written in the Devanagari script). As a result of the marginalization of Urdu, writers who continued to write in it and publishers who published in it were similarly marginalized.

Publishing in Gujarati

In other parts of India, publishing in Indian languages took a different route. In Gujarat, in western India, for example, Gujarati publishing went through a sort of renaissance as a result of the involvement of M.K. Gandhi, the father of Indian independence. Gujarati was Gandhi's mother tongue and he chose to use a simple, colloquial form both in his speeches and in his writings. He was prolific in his writings and his publication office and printing unit, Navjivan Press, gradually turned into a publishing house focusing mainly on his work. These were published in large numbers immediately after independence and continue to be published to this day at affordable prices.

Like Gandhi, other individuals who took an interest in publishing were to influence the development of publishing in this language. A number of charitable trusts were set up that took on the task of publishing books at lower prices and sold these in innovative ways through subscriptions, door-to-door sales, and so on. The Lok Milap Trust, set up in the late 1960s, was known for publishing books with print runs that ran into the hundreds of thousands. Its founder, Mahendra Meghani, began by piling books on a cart and selling them in public areas. Now in his seventies, Meghani continues to carry books to villages, an enterprise in which he is assisted by his children. These efforts have helped to popularize books in Gujarat. Unfortunately, these have remained isolated efforts. A much more intractable problem, for example, is that despite—the existence of a good library network in Gujarat, and particularly in its villages—there has been little benefit to publishers because libraries have no funds to meet their expenses or to purchase books.

PUBLISHING IN MARATHI

In Marathi, Gujarati's sister language from the neighboring state of Maharashtra, modern day publishing received its initial impetus from the efforts of major British publishers, such as Oxford University Press, Blackie, and Macmillan, which published textbooks in English and Marathi from their base in the state capital, Bombay. In the early years, because the language of education was Marathi, indigenous language publishers were able to produce better books than the British publishing houses; they therefore used this opportunity intelligently to build a solid base in publishing. Thus, although they did suffer some setbacks when this market was taken away from them, they were not as badly affected as publishers in other parts of India. What did affect indigenous language publishing in this state, however, was the rise in the cost of printing and production as a result of progressive labor laws and consequent rises in labor costs.

Other developments were to impinge on publishing in Marathi. After Maharashtra was created as a linguistic state in 1960, the government set up a State Board for Literature and Culture. It was the mandate of this organization to publish books but also to buy books in large quantities at subsidized prices from private sector publishers, and then to offer these at lower prices in the market. Despite these and other innovative developments, the shortage of bookselling outlets in the country remained a major hurdle in the development of publishing. Experiments by individuals or groups—such as the movement called Granthali, which took books to rural areas with the help of university professors and students—showed that it was possible to sell books in places far and wide. But these remained isolated incidents.

PUBLISHING IN HINDI

Hindi speakers form the largest language group in India, covering about

40 percent of the population of some 800 million. Hindi publishers estimate that books in this language make up at least 25 percent of the books published in India every year and are very skeptical of any figures that say otherwise. Hindi publishers were particularly active in producing books and pamphlets at the time of independence and this first flush of enthusiasm sustained them for many years afterwards. Although publishing in Hindi remained hampered by the same kinds of problems that other languages faced, it was in this language, too, that the experiment of setting up book clubs was most successful. Gharelu Library Yojana (the Home Library Plan), whose membership ran to some 50,000 subscribers, was the name of the book club set up by Hind Pocket Books to popularize books in Hindi.

However, the market for each language in India is unique and has its own problems and constraints. In Hindi, the government's role in bulk purchase of books acted as a barrier to publishers experimenting with new areas; many of them preferred to play it safe and stick with the kinds of books they knew would come under such bulk purchase schemes. In addition, the absence of a network of libraries and bookshops meant that publishers had to rely on the mail to send their books to different areas. Postal rates remained consistently high, and matters got worse for Hindi publishers due to the pressure from distributors and wholesalers for higher discounts.

Despite these difficulties, Hindi publishing has managed to survive and to produce some excellent books. In recent years, a number of bookshops, at least in metropolitan areas in the Hindi-speaking areas, have started to carry Hindi books. In time, this may help to improve the distribution of these books.

Publishing in Malayalam

In other parts of India where the conditions have been conducive for publishing, the results have been impressive. Kerala, in southern India, is a state that has been, for the most part, under communist rule for the last several decades. As a result of a vigorous campaign to promote literacy and education, Kerala has almost 100 percent literacy. In the 1940s, a library movement was started in Kerala through which libraries were organized at the village level and every village was equipped with a library and a reading room. As a result of this initial impetus, and the state's high literacy rate, there is an ongoing need for reading materials in Kerala; the spread of village libraries has helped to service this need. Today, a little more than half a century after the inception of the library movement, there are some 4,000 village libraries in Kerala. Unlike libraries in many other parts of India, Kerala's village libraries continue to receive grants for the purchase of books each year. In addition, there are also a large number of public libraries in Kerala that buy books, which helps to sustain publishing in the state.

The 1940s also saw another unique development in Kerala: the setting up of an authors' cooperative society known as the Sahitya Pravartak Cooperative Society (SPCS). With a small membership and a paid up dues of 120 rupees (about US$3 at 1990s rates), the Society was slow to develop in the early stages, but soon took off to become one of the most important book cooperative developments not only in India but internationally. In its first four years, the Society published only one book and increased its dues by 40 rupees (US$1). It was only when it went into partnership with National Book Stall (NBS), a distribution company with outlets all over Kerala, that things began to change. Soon a growing number of books were produced—printed by the Society's own printing division—and sold through NBS outlets. As the situation improved, membership went up and SPCS was able to increase its capital base, as well as pay authors unusually high royalties—up to 25 percent. In 1965, the government recognized the SPCS as one of the 12 best cooperative societies in India. Books were sold through subscriptions, installments, prepublication offers, and a number of other innovative methods, and showrooms were set up in different places. At the time, the SPCS did so well that its fame spread far and wide and it came to be seen as a model for other publishers. Virtually every well-known author in Kerala was associated with it, and the Society spawned at least 13 other similar efforts.

With the decline of the cooperative movement after the mid-1970s, SPCS operations also began to decrease. Several of its members set up their own publishing and distribution units, gaining from the experience of the SPCS and profiting, also, from the generally good state of literacy and education in the state. Today, some of these publishers are among the leading names in Malayalam publishing. A more recent entrant to the Malayalam publishing scene is a nongovernmental organization called the Kerala Sastra Sahitya Parishad (KSSP), whose members are mostly university students and teachers. KSSP members travel on foot, by bicycle, and by boat across Kerala in an attempt to inculcate a "rational" and "scientific" temperament among people. One of the principal ways in which they do this is through the sale and distribution of books. It is because of the combination of circumstances described above that Kerala continues to be one of the most healthy and vibrant publishing states in India.

Publishing in Tamil

Literacy, by contrast, is low in the southern state of Tamil Nadu and not much effort has been put into developing reading habits there. Thus, despite the fact that Tamil is among the oldest languages and has a rich tradition of classical literature, Tamil publishing does not have the same kind of vibrancy and reach as Malayalam does. However, in terms of infrastructure, Tamil Nadu has a fairly extensive library network, with 2,547 libraries. It was also the first state to introduce the Public Library Act, although the functioning of these libraries often leaves a great deal to be desired. Most of the bookstores spread throughout the state deal with textbooks, although there are a few that stock general and trade books; but, once again, the bulk of these are in English. One of the unique features of Tamil Nadu is that it has a chain of bookstores (Higginbothams) that often sell books through the use of mobile shops, which service areas that are some distance away from their bookshops.

Publishing in Telugu

Tamil's sister language, Telugu, spoken in the state of Andhra Pradesh, is another language rich in its variety of literature. The Telugu literary scene is lively, but many of the books by new writers are often published by small groups of interested people or individuals. Indeed, this entry of voluntary organizations and small political groups as publishers is unique to Telugu publishing. As an organized activity, Telugu publishing concentrates, like many other Indian languages, on textbooks, although some general books—particularly literary books—do get published. The state of Andhra Pradesh has an excellent public library system that spreads far and wide. All districts have a major district library and there are 1,424 branch libraries covering a large area. In addition, there are other government-owned libraries. These libraries purchase multiple copies of titles—each running into hundreds—and total purchases can be as much as 1 million rupees annually. These purchases notwithstanding, the lack of retail outlets—something that has begun to change recently—works against higher sales, particularly as library grants have declined in recent years.

Publishing in Bengali

Further north, Bengali is one of the largest publishing languages in India. Although Bengal does not boast a very high literacy rate (58 percent), it has very high readership levels and a lively literary scene, with Bengali writings of all sorts being read, reviewed, and discussed. Bengal is also unique in that some of its large business houses, particularly newspaper companies, have set up their own book publishing units and produce a fair number of books for general reading.

The Communist government of West Bengal has played an active role in encouraging Bengali writing and publishing. One of the ways in which this has been done is by providing subsidies to authors. This scheme, launched in the 1980s, has so far given subsidies to some 400 authors. In addition, the government has a comprehensive plan for purchasing books: government and government-aided libraries receive a 100 percent grant from the government for the purchase of books. They are required to spend 30 percent of this on books from a select list prepared by the government and are free to spend the remaining 70 percent on books of their choice. The amount of the grant to libraries is now more than 10 million rupees each year. Government schools and government-aided schools also receive grants for the purchase of books every year. With these assured markets and a rich literary tradition, Bengal is one of the foremost states in quality publishing.

Challenges of Indigenous Publishing

The languages covered above describe only a handful of the many languages of Indian publishing. It is not possible to detail each language, or indeed to do justice to the ones discussed, in this brief space. What these descriptions demonstrate, however, is that although there are vast differences in the state of publishing in the different languages of India, there are also some common problems. For example, it is clear that in those parts of the country where a good library network exists, and where the government has ensured library grants, book sales are healthier than in other areas. Equally, the absence of a reasonable infrastructure of retail bookshops has, by and large, been detrimental to Indian language publishing. This is immediately evident when a comparison with the English language is made: the number of English retail outlets in India far exceeds those for Indian language books.

Another difficulty is that books in Indian languages, for the most part, have maintained lower price levels than books in English. However, increases in the costs of raw material, as well as labor costs, do not differentiate between languages. As a result, Indian language publishers have found it particularly difficult to overcome reader resistance and raise the price of books. Many have compromised by reducing the number of titles and the quantities in which they publish them. Another consequence of rising costs has been that publishers, who are not willing to take risks with higher priced books, have turned only to publishing the kinds of books that they know will be bought by the government through its bulk purchase schemes.

Such schemes exist in almost every state, and were set up to help indigenous language publishing grow. Today, as the market for books becomes smaller, due to price increases and fewer library grants, bulk purchases by the government are often the only means of survival for some publishers.

The constant need to reduce budgets has not been very encouraging. Earlier after independence, authors often involved themselves in the development and production of their books, sometimes acting as editors. More recently, this relationship has become more distant and authors are not as directly involved in the process of publishing. The impact of these developments is reflected in the poor quality of books. Very few publishers, however, have found it necessary to compensate for this by hiring professionals, such as editors. Furthermore, with the exception of a few languages such as Malayalam, Bengali, and Tamil, where newspapers and magazines devote considerable space to books, most Indian language newspapers and magazines pay little attention to books. Without exposure in the media, it becomes even more difficult to sell books.

For many years now, publishers in India have been lobbying on a number of issues. Key among these are the need for cheaper postal rates for books and the opening up of paper imports. India is one of the few developing countries that manufactures a substantial amount of its own paper. Often, extreme shortages of paper in the market occur, due to, for example, natural disasters, such as floods that affect the supply of paper, and man-made "disasters," such as frequent election campaigns that use large quantities of paper. These contribute to sharp increases in prices. Once the crisis is over, prices seldom go down. Because of the kind of tight budgets on which Indian language publishers work, they are then forced to buy cheaper quality paper, compromising further the quality of their books.

Another major problem has to do with the size of the country: even if it were possible to translate books from one Indian language to another directly—without going through the medium of Hindi or English—it would be difficult to send books all over the country. Currently, most publishers use the already overstretched railway freight system, the mail, or road transport, though the last takes longer and is often less reliable, particularly when the weather is not good. The only "safe" and quick alternative is to distribute books to different parts of the country by air, but this is virtually impossible for the Indian language publisher.

Overall, however, the picture of publishing in Indian languages is quite varied. Nothing is more indicative of the success of Bengali publishing, for example, than the long queues of people waiting to buy books at the annual Calcutta Book Fair. It is well known that people in Bengal save all year round in order to afford the books of their choice offered at the fair.

At the same time, nothing could be further from this picture than the state of publishing in neighboring Assam, or indeed across the country in Kashmir. Not only are their literacy levels lower than in Bengal, but both states have been riven with political unrest and militancy for several years now. The fledgling publishing industry has had virtually no opportunity to grow. Educational institutions are often closed. "Normal" bookselling activity, such as bookfairs and exhibitions, rarely takes place, and there are virtually no bookshops left. A further disincentive is that publishers cannot allow themselves to be seen as successful for fear of extortion by the militants. Effectively, then, publishing in these strife-torn states hardly exists.

Future Trends

Despite some positive signs, the future of Indian language publishing is somewhat uncertain. Over the years, print runs of books have decreased, partly because of the rise in prices and the overall increase in the cost of living. These trends, however, are common to publishing the world over. What is unique to India is the attention and importance that is attached to publishing in English. In recent years, Indian authors have been much sought after internationally. Several of the younger English writers, such as Arundhati Roy, Vikram Seth, Vikram Chandra, Amit Chaudhuri, and, more recently, Ruchir Joshi, Githa Hariharan, Manjula Padmanabhan, and Pankaj Misra, to name a few, have been paid large sums of money as advances for their creative writing. As a result, the home market has become much more receptive to these, and other, writers. Indeed, new writers who choose the same language receive much more media attention than do writers in the other Indian languages. Increasingly, the spotlight on English makes publishing in other Indian languages pale by comparison, particularly as the payment of large advances is accompanied by a great deal of fanfare and publicity—something which the poorly financed Indian language publisher can not afford.

Although a novel by a Hindi writer, or one writing in Marathi, Malayalam, Bengali, or another Indian language, may actually sell more copies than, say, a book by an English language writer, the return to the former will be much less than that earned by the latter. Often, however, while books in Indian languages may not find a lucrative market among the reading public, they do serve as a rich base for television broadcasting; in some languages, magazines and newspapers that have large circulations provide considerable space for the work of new writers. These are some of the less direct ways in which the work of new writers reaches the reading public.

Another factor that has affected Indian language publishing negatively is the increasing reliance of some publishers on government grants. This has led to apathy rather than innovation and creativity. Nevertheless, those publishers who have attempted to break through have met with considerable success, as books in Malayalam, Bengali, Marathi, and Hindi have found huge markets. The two government organizations involved with books that publish in Indian languages, the National Book Trust and the Sahitya Akademi, have also had very positive responses to their books. Indeed, the Akademi's awards for translations and literary works have inspired many Indian language writers and helped popularize them outside their particular states. Distribution and dissemination of books by the Akademi, however, leave a great deal to be desired. Equally, the National Book Trust's regional book fairs, organized in different parts of the country, provide a forum for Indian language books of all kinds, are usually extremely well attended, and have cash sales that make most publishers come back year after year with more books. In addition, the World Book Fair, organized every two years in Delhi by the National Book Trust, has seen more and more space being devoted to books in the Indian languages, and the buildings housing these publishers are crowded from the first day. On occasion, publishers have themselves underestimated this market, not bringing enough stock to sell.

Clearly, there is a need to develop this very important area of publishing in India. There is little doubt that there are good writers and willing readers. What is lacking, however, is the infrastructure in terms of retail outlets, cheap postal rates, easy availability of reasonably priced paper, and, of course, most importantly, the will to improve and develop these areas. This is a situation in which the initiative and drive can only come from publishers themselves. Hopefully, they will attend to these issues in the not too distant future.

Note

1. At present, for example, statistics for the number of titles published annually are compiled on the basis of books sent under the Delivery of Books (Public Libraries) Act of 1954. This act requires all publishers to send out four copies of each title published by them to a number of public libraries in the country. It is well known that a large number of publishers do not send these mandatory copies. Failure to do so normally involves a small fine, which is seldom levied. Thus, when statistics are compiled from those books that are sent in, there is no way of knowing how accurate they

are. Accuracy apart, however, the broad pattern described by the above statistics is accepted, albeit somewhat reluctantly, by many publishers. Despite the apparent need, there has been no attempt to conduct a similar survey, other than a privately commissioned one by the British Council whose findings are confidential. *Survey of the Indian Book Industry*, Vols. 1 and 2, Delhi, National Council of Applied Economic Research.

8

World or Indigenous Languages? Influences on Language Policies for Publishing in Africa

Thomas Clayton

Introduction

In 1997, the winner, the runner-up, and the three honorable mentions for the Noma Prize were written and published in English, Portuguese, and English, respectively.[1] Why were the books chosen for this prize established to honor indigenously published African authors written and published in world languages, as opposed to indigenous African languages? In fact, given the vigorous advocacy on behalf of indigenous languages by such noted African authors as Ngugi wa Thiong'o and Ousmane Sembène, why are the vast majority of the books produced in and for use in Africa written in world languages?[2] In order to suggest an answer to this complex question, this chapter examines historical and contemporary influences on language policies for publishing in Africa. Following Chinua Achebe's example, in this chapter I refer to languages such as English, French, and Portuguese as "world" languages, though these languages may be referred to as European languages, metropolitan languages, *lingua franca*e and languages of wider communication elsewhere in language policy literature.[3]

National Influences on Language of Publication

Language policy decisions in publishing are not made in a vacuum. Indeed, authors make decisions about languages in which to write and publishers make decisions about languages in which to produce books, journals, newspapers, and texts against a backdrop of complex and often contradictory influences. Influences may originate within nations;

writers and publishers may make language decisions in response to these national goals and constraints.

NATIONAL INTEGRATION

At a meeting in Berlin in 1884, the great European powers dispassionately carved Africa into colonies. While attention was given to the location of specific European national economic and missionary outposts, little attention was paid to traditional ethnic and linguistic boundaries in Africa. Thus, African colonies and the nations they became at independence were and often remain fantastically multiethnic and multilingual. In Nigeria, for example, more than 250 languages are spoken; in contrast, Mali's 11 indigenous languages seem few.[4]

At independence, language was one of many difficult issues facing Africa's new national governments. During the colonial period, European languages had been used widely in domains such as education, administration, and the courts, and these languages had provided the medium through which Africans could communicate not only with Europeans, but also with other Africans from different linguistic groups located within the same colonial empires. As the colonial era ended, African policy makers realized a common language served an important function by providing a linguistic vehicle for the integration of many ethnic and linguistic groups into a single, national entity.[5] Policy makers also realized from hard experience that selecting an indigenous language for this purpose might lead to ethnic conflict. In the late 1970s in Mali, for instance, Fulbe speakers threatened to burn down a Bambara language literacy center because they feared an increased instrumentality for Bambara would devalue their own language in the community.[6] Similar language policy conflicts erupted in India, Malaysia, and South Africa, to name but a few locations.[7]

In the face of these national goals and constraints, many African governments elected to retain colonial languages for national purposes after independence, arguing that use of these world languages would facilitate the integration of linguistically diverse populations without privileging particular groups and engendering the animosity of others. Of course, postcolonial world language policies have had an impact on publication, as writers and publishers—particularly those engaged in the production of texts for educational systems governed by national language policies—have written and published in world languages. South African writer Ezekiel Mphahlete, discussing the importance for African writers of postcolonial national integration projects and their historical roots, concludes that "colonialism . . .

provided [African writers] with a common language" with which to negotiate postcolonial multilingualism.[8]

ELITE CLOSURE

If world language policies after independence were intended to facilitate national integration, it is relevant to ask whether they have been effective in drawing diverse populations together in African nations. In fact, scholars conclude unequivocally that they have not. Despite years of support for world languages in education and other domains throughout Africa, scholars estimate that only 10 to 20 percent of Africans are competent in those languages.[9] While it is not reasonable to expect that mass integration would result from a policy that has affected so few, another outcome has been noted. As linguist Eyamba Bokamba observes, "English, French, and Portuguese in the case of Africa have produced each a distinct élite ... that receives most of the benefits while the non-speakers of these languages have been and continue to be marginalized."[10]

While Bokamba sees social stratification as an unintended result of Africa's world language policies, other scholars discern a different causative pattern. Linguist Carol Meyers Scotton, for instance, argues that world language policies in Africa were established at independence and have been supported ever since by elites intent upon maintaining their social, political, and economic positions at the expense of others. As Scotton correctly points out, competence in world languages is "necessary for participation in situations which yield power" in postcolonial Africa.[11] Since education is the primary venue for the acquisition of world languages, she continues, and since education remains an elite institution in much of Africa, elites are able to engineer a distinct sociolinguistic stratification and a "closure" on access to power through their support for world language policies. Scotton concludes: "socioeconomic mobility and political power [are limited to elites who have] educational and social opportunities [to acquire] the requisite linguistic patterns," while nonelites who do not have access to education and, as a result, are not competent in world languages, are denied these opportunities.[12]

The boundary created and maintained between classes by world language polices in Africa is, of course, not impermeable. Indeed, as Ngugi wa Thiong'o's own history illustrates, it is entirely possible for Africans of modest means to enroll and succeed in schools, to acquire world languages, and ultimately to gain entry to those "situations which yield power."[13] This potential for upward mobility exerts a strong influence on language preferences among Africans. In education, students and parents tend to demonstrate positive attitudes toward world languages, accurately concluding that their future opportunities depend on their competency in them. Linguist Olascope Oyelaran, for example, argues that "Nigerians would sacrifice anything to acquire English [since it is seen as] the *key* to material well-being."[14] African writers and publishers are also affected, responding to popular demand by writing and publishing in world languages despite the fact that "the use of metropolitan languages in publishing... gives [elites, often including the writers and publishers themselves] considerable advantage over the majority of the population."[15]

CHALLENGING APARTHEID STRUCTURES

If world language policies are used by elites in some African nations to facilitate inequitable social stratification, society's dominant class has used a diverse language policy structure to achieve the same ends in other African nations. Under apartheid, the governments of South Africa and Namibia pursued policies of separation for the white minority and the nonwhite majority. The most obvious of these policies was, of course, physical segregation. Separation was also attempted, however, through language policies. The apartheid government "used language differences [among ethnic groups] to create ethnic divisiveness attempt[ing] to drive the people to focus on linguo-tribal affiliations and differences instead of national unity."[16] As the future Prime Minister of Namibia, Hage G. Geingob, stated in 1981, "South Africa has always pursued a deliberate policy of ethnolinguistic fragmentation in order to divide the people of Namibia."[17] Dennis Brutus agrees about South Africa itself, concluding in 1981 that the "apartheid government... has tried [through language policies and other means] to revive the old tribal structures" and thus divide South Africans against both themselves and the white minority.[18]

Like nonelite Africans in elite closure situations, nonwhite southern Africans were blocked from opportunities as a result of language policies dictated by others, in this case the apartheid regime. As Brutus argues, emphasis on indigenous languages in education and elsewhere denied South Africans knowledge of English, the world language associated with social, economic, and political opportunity in the region, and thus "prevent[ed] them from participating in the present political [etc.] process[es]."[19] According to Caroline Kerfoot, an English teacher in southern Africa, the adult literacy students with whom she works are "well aware of how lack of proficiency in English effectively silence[s] them and prevent[s] them from obtaining information, claiming rights, or resisting exploitation."[20]

In anticipation of the political changes of the early 1990s, South Africans and Namibians launched world language policy initiatives in the 1980s. In 1981, the Namibian South West Africa People's Organization named English the official language; in South Africa, the National Education Crisis Committee initiated the People's English Movement, an educational enterprise dedicated to the promotion of English among nonwhite South Africans, in 1986.[21] In both cases, Africans saw competency in English as essential to the broader participation of nonwhites in social, economic, and political life.[22] African writers and publishers have taken an active role in this democratic movement in southern Africa. Ezekiel Mphahlete, for instance, gave permission for his English language book *Down Second Avenue* to be adapted as a text for the People's English Movement. That this movement intends revolutionary social change is evident in the publisher's introduction to *Down Second Avenue*, in which the South African Council of Higher Education explains its commitment to "counter[ing] the imbalance created by the apartheid education system."[23]

FINANCIAL CONSTRAINTS

If integrating diverse populations, restricting opportunities, and challenging apartheid structures are potential outcomes of world language policies in Africa, these policies themselves are often the outcome of a particular national constraint—notably, the scarcity of financial resources. Because European languages were used in Africa during the colonial period, structures often did not exist at independence to support the use of other languages. Specifically, indigenous languages often had not been developed sufficiently—in terms of script codification, dialect and spelling system standardization, and vocabulary elaboration—for broad postcolonial use.[24] At independence, the costs for the new national governments of developing one or more indigenous languages, writing and publishing new materials in these languages for national purposes, and training educators to teach these languages in schools were often deemed prohibitively expensive, and European languages were retained by default. In explaining the decision to maintain an English language policy for Kenya's legal system, for example, a Kenyan government official pointed to "the insurmountable practical difficulties in translating our laws and other legal and quasi-legal documents into Swahili" and other indigenous languages.[25]

In addition to the costs involved in developing the infrastructure to print materials in scripts other than the roman alphabet, African writers and publishers face another financial constraint which militates against the use of indigenous languages: the size of indigenous language markets in relation to those of world languages. Publishers realize that producing books for the hundreds or thousands of speech communities in African translates into a "smaller . . . readership for any given language version [and a] greater . . . cost per book."[26] Writers also grasp linguistic economies of scale. Before forsaking French, Senegalese writer Ousmane Sembène explained why he wrote his novel *Le Docker Noir* in that language. If he had written in Wolof, his native language, he observed, "who would have read it? How many people know how to read the language? . . . Even written in French, how many Africans have read *Le Docker Noir?* Eighty-five percent of the people here are illiterate; the rest can read and write but they do not read African authors. That means that our public is in Europe."[27]

Given the thin line between profit and insolvency in publishing in Africa, and the necessity for authors to make enough money to support themselves, many publishers and writers in Africa work pragmatically in world languages because those languages allow them to access larger markets.[28]

DECOLONIZING THE MIND

Thus far, we have seen that the use of world languages in publishing and other domains in Africa may facilitate social engineering at the national level (whether integration, stratification, or revolutionary restructuring) and may respond to national financial constraints. Beyond these influences supporting writing and publishing in world languages are important influences encouraging the greater use of indigenous languages.

Ngugi wa Thiong'o is perhaps the most vocal advocate for indigenous language use in Africa. Educated in colonial Kenya, Ngugi achieved international acclaim for a series of English language novels published in the 1960s and 1970s. In 1977, however, Ngugi abandoned English as the medium for creative writing in favor of Gikuyu, his native language. He was jailed by Kenyan authorities after the production in 1977 of the play *Ngaahika Ndeenda* (*I Will Marry When I Want*), written in Gikuyu with Ngugi wa Mirii.[29] Since that time, Ngugi has reserved English for what he calls his "explanatory prose," notably his influential *Decolonising the Mind: The Politics of Language in African Literature*.[30]

For Ngugi and others, such as Senegalese writer Ousmane Sembène, indigenous languages are, first and foremost, the most appropriate medium for communication with other Africans on African matters. Given that the vast majority of Africans do not command world languages and thus cannot read literature in these languages, these authors argue, writers should accommodate themselves to their compatriots through personal language policy choices. In 1979, for instance, after seeing the lack of impact his French language films had on village audiences, Sembène realized, "if I wanted to make films for my people, then it must be in their language."³¹ Ngugi reached a similar conclusion about audience in 1976, when he became involved in a community education program. Participation in this project, he writes, "forced me to turn to Gikuyu and hence into what for me has amounted to 'an epistemological break' with my [English language] past. The question of audience settled the problem of language choice; and the language choice settled the question of audience."³²

But for Ngugi, in particular, writing in indigenous languages has broader implications than appropriate communication with fellow Africans. It also challenges structures of alienation inherited from the colonial period. Under British rule, he writes, "Kenyan languages ... were associated with negative qualities of backwardness, underdevelopment, humiliation, and punishment." Those educated in colonial schools, he continues, "were meant to graduate with a hatred of the people and the culture and the values of the language of our daily humiliation and punishment." By producing a literature in indigenous languages in the postcolonial period, Ngugi concludes, those languages will gain value for Africans in relation to world languages, and Africans will escape the "tradition of contempt for the tools of communication developed by their communities and their history."³³ Replacing world languages with indigenous languages in publishing, education, and other domains in Africa is thus central for Ngugi to achieving psychological independence from alienating structures of the past—that is, to "decolonizing the minds" of contemporary Africans.

LINGUISTIC INTERDEPENDENCE

Ngugi's project has received indirect support from several non-African scholars interested in what they term "linguistic human rights." Equating the right to use one's first language with rights such as freedom of speech and religion, linguists Tove Skutnabb-Kangas, Robert Phillipson, and others argue that all people should be able to use their own languages to communicate with their governments in the courts, the polls, and other official domains, to study in schools, and to express themselves creatively.³⁴ Like Ngugi, these scholars advocate on behalf of groups whose languages historically have been marginalized and devalued in relation to other languages—Sami speakers in Scandinavia, for instance, or Kurdish speakers in Turkey—and thus see their enterprise as part of a larger process of social democratization.[35]

This ethical argument in favor of the valorization of indigenous languages is supported by much educational research into what linguist Jim Cummins terms the "linguistic interdependence principle."[36] In general, Cummins' and related research shows that students are able to apply certain aspects of literacy in one language to other languages.[37] Cummins explains, "although the surface aspects (e.g., pronunciation...) of different languages are clearly separate, there is an underlying cognitive/academic proficiency which is common across languages. This [proficiency] makes possible the transfer of cognitive, academic or literacy related skills across language."[38] For Cummins, these findings have clear implications for language policies in educational programs for minority language students. These students, he argues, should first gain literacy in their native languages, as this proficiency will subsequently facilitate literacy in the majority language of their setting. Among Spanish speakers in the United States, for instance, he concludes, "Spanish instruction that develops Spanish reading and writing skills... is not just developing *Spanish* skills, it is also developing a deeper conceptual and linguistic proficiency that is strongly related to the development of literacy in the majority [English] language."[39]

Educational policy makers in certain African nations have recognized the efficacy of facilitating student literacy in first languages as a transition to literacy in European languages. In Ghana, for example, students study in a variety of indigenous languages for the first several years of school, moving to English language education by the fourth grade.[40] While this form of transitional bilingual education is more common in Anglophone than Francophone Africa, Mali recently experimented successfully with the use of four indigenous languages in initial primary education in anticipation of subsequent education in French.[41] As educational leaders in these and other countries implement indigenous language policies for primary schools, demand, of course, increases for appropriate materials, and African writers and publishers are called upon to produce texts in indigenous languages.

International Influences on Language of Publication

As we have seen, language policies for publishing in Africa are influenced by several goals and constraints at the national level. Influences may additionally flow from outside national boundaries, and the decisions made about language of publication in Africa may respond to these international imperatives.

INTERNATIONAL COMMUNICATION

In his 1981 statement introducing Namibia's English language policy, future Prime Minister Hage G. Geingob explained that his government "had to choose a language that would open up the world to us. English was the obvious choice. After all, English is the most widely spoken language, spoken by some 600 million people. There is no corner of the globe where you could not get by if you knew English."[42]

With this statement, Geingob identified a powerful influence encouraging world language policies not only in Namibia, but throughout Africa—namely, international communication. Because world languages such as English, French, and, to a certain extent, Portuguese are established officially in so many countries, they provide the media through which speakers of myriad native languages can communicate in diplomacy, business, higher education, and other domains. Of primary importance to many African policy makers is the ability to follow advances in science and technology published in journals or presented at conferences where world languages predominate.[43] Linguist Catherine Griefenow-Mewis, for example, explains that "the growing gap between the developing countries and the leading industrialized nations has been [cited] by African intellectuals . . . who are concerned that the increased usage of African languages in education would exclude the African states from international developments in science and technology . . . because scientific publications are published mainly in English or French."[44]

Many scholars interested in the international dissemination of knowledge argue that information tends to flow into, rather than out of, Africa.[45] To the extent that Africans contribute to world knowledge, however, they generally do so in world languages. For writer Lewis Nkosi, world languages allow African authors to "interpret . . . a continent to the world"—that is, to explain African cultures, conflicts, and issues to an international audience that otherwise would not have access to genuine African perspectives.[46] Ngugi wa Thiong'o agrees, at least historically, arguing that world languages permitted Africa's first generation of postcolonial writers to describe colonial inequities and independence struggles to an international audience and thus to contribute to "that great anti-colonial and anti-imperialist upheaval in . . . Africa" and elsewhere.[47] Outside the African context, Pin Yathay's French language memoir, *L'Utopie Meurtrière: Un Rescapé du Génocide Cambodgien Témoigne*, is widely credited with bringing information about the Khmer Rouge's "murderous utopia" to international attention and with turning public opinion against that regime's successors.[48]

WORLD-SYSTEM RELATIONS

In a recent volume, Philip Altbach argues that there is "considerable inequality in world publishing." As Altbach correctly points out, a few countries, among them the United States, Great Britain, France, and Germany, control the vast majority of the world's book production; in contrast, "most of the rest of the world is peripheral to [these] major centers of publishing."[49] Altbach and Eva Rathgeber make a similar argument in an earlier volume, suggesting that "Third World nations are at a distinct disadvantage in the international publishing system [being] dependent on the industrialized nations, which hold the bulk of the world's resources, particularly in the areas that impinge on books and publishing."[50]

With these comments, Altbach discusses a complex body of literature about the international flow of capital and introduces a powerful influence on language policies in Africa—specifically, the inequitable relations among core and periphery nations in the capitalist world-system. Though Altbach applies world-system terms and concepts to publishing, world-systems theory was originally an economic construct proposed by Immanuel Wallerstein to explain the global expansion of capitalism.[51] For Wallerstein, "core" and "periphery" nations have historically struggled with one another for scarce global resources in much the same way that, for Marxist scholars, classes grapple with one another in individual societies.[52]

In economic history, according to Wallerstein, core and periphery are points of shifting geographical location, as nations rise and fall in economic power over time and in relation to one another. During the colonial era, European powers established international economic networks in the form of colonial regimes; these colonial systems were based on an "unequal exchange of goods and services, such that much of the surplus-value extracted in the periphery zones [that is, the colonies, was] transferred to the core zones [that is, the metropoles]."[53] After colonial independence in the mid-twentieth century, two important processes shaped the contemporary world-system. First, European powers attempted to maintain dependency relations with former colonies through new, neocolonial structures. As Francis MacNamara comments, for example, colonial administrators throughout Francophone Africa simply moved into newly built French embassies as ambassadors or "exchanged colonial gold braid for business suits and the anonymity of titles like advisor."[54]

Second, while European powers struggled to maintain their colonial empires, a new generation of nations and blocs of nations began to rise in international economic power. The United States, Japan, the Cold War ideological blocs, and the contemporary international economic communities established themselves as cores to new sets of peripheries, and capital began to flow within these new economic systems while continuing to flow within systems established by colonialism in the nineteenth century. The contemporary world-system, then, comprises a variety of cores—some national and some transnational, some waxing in power and some waning—engaged with a variety of peripheries (many subordinate to multiple cores) in an unequal exchange of global resources.[55] In this world-system, African nations remain peripheral to former colonial powers, while also assuming periphery status in relation to more recent world economic powers.

Africa's position in the contemporary world-system has a number of implications for publishing generally and for language policies more specifically. As many scholars point out, the majority of the world's publishing companies are located in core nations, while Africa's publishing infrastructure remains extremely limited.[56] As a result, African nations "are basically dependent on the industrialized [core] nations" for books and other published materials.[57] Whether or not core enterprises purposefully undermine periphery publishing ventures so as to maintain control over the means of world publishing production, this dependency relationship is advantageous to core publishing companies, for which Africa represents a lucrative market.[58] In other words, the unequal distribution of publishing resources in the world-system facilitates the flow of capital from the African periphery to core sites in Europe and North America. Moreover, publishing dependency has a significant impact on language policies in Africa, as the easy availability of high-quality books in world languages from core countries may itself influence language decisions in domains such as education. As Karen Biraimah explains with reference to Togo and other Francophone nations, as long as textbooks are published in France, "the issue of language remains moot."[59]

Beyond "actual" capital, Africa's publishing dependency returns "symbolic" capital to core nations and blocs of nations in the form of adherence to political, economic, and cultural ideologies associated with those nations and blocs. As many scholars note, books provide an ideal medium for the transmission of ideas, particularly in settings like Africa, "where other elements of the mass media, such as television, may be limited."[60] If books are produced nationally and imbued with "values . . . in which the country's leadership wishes to inculcate its younger generations," these ideologies may have effects that advance national goals.[61] If produced by core publishing companies, however, books may transmit ways of thinking associated with core nation or blocs. In her analysis of Togo's school texts produced in France, for instance, Karen Biraimah found "gender-specific messages [that] did not conform to [indigenous] labor force participation patterns."[62] Whether the promotion of core ideologies in periphery settings is intentional or not, the valorization in books of particular ways of thinking may have the effect of drawing peripheral nations into the political, economic, and cultural orbits of particular core nations or blocs and, thus, of altering or reinforcing world-system relations.[63]

Several scholars see world languages as integral to the movement of symbolic capital in the world-system, particularly within orbits controlled by individual core nations; for these scholars, world languages in books and other media both valorize particular national cultures and serve as conduits for political and economic ideologies associated with those nations. Thus, Robert Phillipson defines the English language as the linchpin in structural relations between Great Britain and the United States, on one hand, and various peripheries, on the other.[64] It is important to note, however, that world languages are not central to all international structural relationships—particularly those sought by core groups dedicated to transnational ideologies. Christian missionaries from many core nations, for example, have been involved for generations in peripheral countries in developing indigenous languages, publishing Bibles in the most accessible media.[65] The Ford Foundation, associated with several scholars in the Western-bloc Cold War project, has also worked extensively in peripheral countries in the production of indigenous language texts and other materials.[66] Finally, nongovernmental organizations based in core nations have frequently expressed their commitment to human rights and social equity through advocacy for indigenous languages in publishing and other domains in the periphery.[67]

Language Policies for Publishing in Africa

This chapter opened with a question: why are the vast majority of the books published in and for use in Africa written in world languages, as opposed to indigenous languages? As we have now seen, language policies for publishing result from a complex array of influences. At the national level, the use of world languages in publishing may intend support national integration, stratification, or revolutionary social change, or it may respond to financial constraints. The use of indigenous languages, on the other hand, may be expected to counteract structures of alienation inherited from the colonial era or to improve educational efficacy. At the international level, world language policies may anticipate international communication; while world language policies may facilitate the extraction of real capital to the benefit of core nations and blocs in the world-system, both world and indigenous languages in publishing may also encourage the international flow of symbolic capital to the benefit of core groups with varying ideological goals.

Of course, language policies for publishing are not established on the basis of one influence in isolation from others. Rather, various configurations of influences reflecting the unique goals, constraints, and imperatives in individual African nations, in particular international structural relationships, comprise the context for language policy decisions. At the present time, these configurations favor world languages in most African nations; as a result, most books published in and for Africa are written in world languages. There is no reason, however, to imagine that current patterns are immutable. Indeed, as contributors to this volume illustrate, important indigenous language publishing ventures are currently under way across the continent. As new influences on language of publication arise, or as the relative power of current influences shift, world language policies may well give way to the greater use of indigenous languages in publishing in and for Africa.

Notes

1. "Ghanaian History Book Wins 1997 Noma Award," *Bellagio Publishing Network Newsletter* 20 (Autumn 1997): 11.

2. On the preponderance of world languages in publishing in Africa, see Philip G. Altbach, "Publishing in the Third World: Issues and Trends for the Twenty-First Century," in *Publishing and Development: A Book of Readings*, eds. Philip G. Altbach and Damtew Teferra (Oxford: Bellagio Publishing Network, 1998), 159–90.

3. Chinua Achebe, "The African Writer and the English Language," in *Morning Yet on Creation Day* (Garden City, NY: Anchor Press, 1975), 91–103.

4. *African Community Languages and Their Use in Literacy and Education* (Dakar: UNESCO, 1985).

5. For discussions of language and national integration, see David Laitin, *Language Repertoires and State Reconstruction in Africa* (Cambridge: Cambridge University Press, 1992); Martin Pütz, ed., *Discrimination Through Language in Africa: Perspectives on the Namibian Experience* (Berlin: Mouton de Gruyter, 1995); and Brian Weinstein, ed., *Language Policy and Political Development* (Norwood, NJ: Ablex Publishing Corporation, 1990).

6. Brian Weinstein, "Language Planning in Francophone Africa," *Language Problems and Language Planning* 4 (Spring 1980): 56–75.

7. Respectively, Philip G. Altbach, "Publishing in the Third World"; Keith Watson, "Cultural Pluralism, Nation-Building, and Educational Policies in Peninsular Malaysia," in *Language Planning and Language Education*, ed. Chris Kennedy (London: George Allen and Unwin, 1984), 132–50; and Bronwyn N. Peirce, "Toward a Pedagogy of Possibility in the Teaching of English Internationally: People's English in South Africa," *TESOL Quarterly* 23 (September 1989): 401–20.

8. Ezekiel Mphahlete, "Polemics: The Dead End of African Literature," *Transition* 3, no. 11 (1963): 8.

9. See, respectively, Aleksandr D. Shveitser and L.B. Nikol'skij, *Introduction to Sociolinguistics* (Amsterdam: John Benjamins Publishing Company, 1986); Bernd Heine, "Language, Language Policy, and National Unity in Africa: An Overview," *Logos* 12, nos. 1–2 (1992): 21–32.

10. Eyamba Bokamba, "The Politics of Language Planning in Africa: Critical Choices for the 21st Century," in *Discrimination Through Language in Africa*, 19.

11. Carol Meyers Scotton, "Elite Closure as Boundary Maintenance: The Case of Africa," in *Language Policy and Political Development*, 25.

12. Scotton, 27. For other discussions of elite closure in Africa, see Jean F. O'Barr, "Language and Politics in Tanzanian Governmental Institutions," in *Language and Politics*, eds. William O. O'Barr and Jean F. O'Barr (The Hague: Mouton, 1976), 69–84; Olascope Oyelaran, "Language, Marginalization, and National Development in Nigeria," in *Multilingualism, Minority Languages, and Language Policy in Nigeria*, ed. E. Nolue Emenanjo (Agbor, Nigeria: Central Books, 1990), 20–30.

13. Ngugi wa Thiong'o, *Decolonising the Mind: The Politics of Language in African Literature* (London: James Currey, 1986).

14. Olascope Oyelaran, "Yoruba as a Medium of Instruction," in *Yoruba Language and Literature*, ed. Adebisi Afolayan (Ibadan: University of Ife Press, 1982), 309; emphasis in the original. On positive attitudes toward world languages in Africa, see Gilbert Ansre, "Four Rationalisations for Maintaining European Languages in Education in Africa," *African Languages* 5, no. 2 (1979): 10–17.

15. Philip G. Altbach and Eva-Marie Rathgeber, *Publishing in the Third World: Trend Report and Bibliography* (New York: Praeger Publishers, 1980), 17.

16. *Toward a Language Policy for Namibia: English as the Official Language: Perspectives and Strategies* (Lusaka: United Nations Institute for Namibia, 1981).

17. Cited in Martin Pütz, "Official Monolingualism in Africa: A Sociolinguistic Assessment of Linguistics and Cultural Pluralism in Namibia," in *Discrimination Through Language in Africa*, 155.

18. Dennis Brutus, "English and the Dynamics of South African Creative Writing," in *English Literature: Opening Up the Canon*, eds. Leslie A. Fiedler and Houston A. Baker (Baltimore: Johns Hopkins University Press, 1981), 11.

19. Ibid.

20. Caroline Kerfoot, "Participatory Education in a South African Context: Contradictions and Challenges," *TESOL Quarterly* 27 (Autumn 1993): 433–34.

21. Respectively, Pütz, "Official Monolingualism in Africa,î and Peirce.

22. See, for example, Hage G. Geingob, "'Our Official Language Shall be English': The Namibian Prime Minister's Perspective," in *Discrimination Through Language in Africa*, 175–79, and Peirce.

23. Cited in Peirce, 414.

24. For a discussion of these language corpus planning processes, see Charles A. Ferguson, "Language Development," in *Language Problems of Developing Nations*, eds. Joshua A. Fishman, Charles A. Ferguson, and Jyotirindra Das Gupta (New York: John Wiley and Sons, 1968), 27–36.

25. Cited in Thomas P. Gorman, "The Development of Language Policy in Kenya with Particular Reference to the Educational System," in *Language in Kenya*, ed. Wilfred H. Whiteley (Nairobi: Oxford University Press, 1974), 438. On financial constraints, also see Björn H. Jernudd, "Notes on Economic Analysis for Solving Language Problems," in *Can Language be Planned? Sociolinguistic Theory and Practice for Developing Nations*, eds. Joan Rubin and Björn H. Jernudd (Honolulu: University Press of Hawaii, 1971), 263–76.

26. Joseph P. Farrell and Stephen P. Heyneman, "Textbooks in Developing Countries: Economic and Pedagogical Choices," in *Textbooks in the Third World: Policy, Content, and Context*, eds. Philip G. Altbach and Gail P. Kelly (New York: Garland Publishing, 1988), 32–33.

27. Comments at a 1963 Francophone writers' conference in Dakar, cited in Oyekan Owomoyela, "The Question of Language in African Literatures," in *A History of Twentieth-Century African Literatures*, ed. Oyekan Owomoyela (Lincoln: University of Nebraska Press, 1993), 354.

28. On the financial situation of publishers in Africa, see Paul Brickhill, "The Transition from State to Commercial Publishing Systems in African Countries," in *Publishing and Development*, 111–30.

29. *Ngaahika Ndeenda* angered Kenyan authorities for several reasons. First, it criticized official government policies by depicting "the transition

of Kenya from a colony with the British interests being dominant to a neo-colony with the doors open to wider imperialist interests from Japan to America" (Ngugi, *Decolonising the Mind*, 44). At least part of the reason for Ngugi's imprisonment, however, was his choice of language. "It is ironic," observes one commentator, "that, while [Ngugi's] earlier English-language works . . . caused controversy and grumbling among those who considered themselves and their class criticized in them, it was when Ngugi turned away from English to Gikuyu to reach his own people . . . that the might of official wrath attempted to silence him" (Arlene A. Elder, "English-Language Fiction From East Africa," in *A History of Twentieth-Century African Literatures*, 79). As Ngugi himself concludes in a veiled reference to the incident, "African languages addressing themselves to the lives of the people become the enemy of a neo-colonial state" (*Decolonising the Mind*, 30). For more on *Ngaahika Ndeenda* and Ngugi's imprisonment, see Ngugi wa Thiong'o, *Detained: A Writer's Prison Diary* (London: Heinemann, 1981).

30. Ngugi, *Decolonising the Mind*, xiv.

31. Cited in Owomoyela, "The Question of Language," 362.

32. Ngugi, *Decolonising the Mind*, 44.

33. Ibid., 28.

34. See Tove Skutnabb-Kangas and Robert Phillipson, *Wanted! Linguistic Human Rights* (Roskilde, Denmark: Roskilde Universitetscenter, 1989); Tove Skutnabb-Kangas, Robert Phillipson, and Mart Rannut, eds., *Linguistic Human Rights: Overcoming Linguistic Discrimination* (Berlin: Mouton de Gruyter, 1994).

35. See Tove Skutnabb-Kangas and Jim Cummins, eds., *Minority Education: From Shame to Struggle* (Clevedon: Multilingual Matters, 1988).

36. For example, Jim Cummins, *Empowering Minority Students* (Sacramento: California Association for Bilingual Education, 1989); and Jim Cummins, "Primary Language Instruction and the Education of Language Minority Students," in *Schooling and Language Minority Students: A Theoretical Framework*, ed. Charles F. Leyba (Los Angeles: University of California Press, 1994), 3–46.

37. In addition to Cummins, see J. Daniel Ramirez, Sandra D. Yuen, and Dena R. Ramey, *Longitudinal Study of Structured English Immersion Strategy, Early-Exit and Late-Exit Transitional Bilingual Education Programs for Language-Minority Children* (San Mateo, CA: Aguire International, 1991); and Tove Skutnabb-Kangas and Pertti Toukomaa, *Teaching Migrant Children's Mother Tongue and Learning the Language of the Host Country in the Context of the Sociocultural Situation of the Migrant Family* (Helsinki: The Finnish National Commission for UNESCO, 1976).

38. Cummins, "Primary Language Instruction," 19.
39. Ibid. Cummins' arguments are not universally accepted; for another perspective, see Rosalie P. Porter, *Forked Tongue: The Politics of Bilingual Education* (New York: Basic Books, 1990).
40. David Laitin and Edward Mensah, "Language Choice Among Ghanaians," *Language Problems and Language Planning* 15 (Summer 1991): 139–61.
41. John Hutchison, *Evaluation of the Experimentation in National Languages in Primary Education in the Republic of Mali* (Washington: United States Agency for International Development, 1990).
42. Geingob, 176.
43. On the predominance of world languages—in particular English—in scientific and technical publications, see Robert B. Kaplan, "The Hegemony of English in Science and Technology," *Journal of Multilingual and Multicultural Development* 14, nos. 1–2 (1993): 151–72.
44. Catherine Griefenow-Mewis, "Status Change of Languages in Sub-Saharan Africa," in *Status Change of Languages*, eds. Ulrich Ammon and Marlis Hellinger (Berlin: Walter de Gruyter, 1992), 119.
45. For example, Philip G. Altbach, *The Knowledge Context: Comparative Perspectives on the Distribution of Knowledge* (Albany: State University of New York Press, 1987).
46. Comments at a 1962 Anglophone writers' conference in Kampala, cited in Owomoyela, "The Question of Language," 353.
47. Ngugi, *Decolonising the Mind*, 21.
48. Pin Yathay, *L'Utopie Meurtrière: Un Rescapé du Génocide Cambodgien Témoigne* (Paris: R. Laffont, 1980).
49. Philip G. Altbach, "Current Trends in Book Publishing," in *Publishing and Development*, 4–5.
50. Altbach and Rathgeber, 11.
51. For example, Immanuel Wallerstein, *The Modern World-System* (New York: Academic Press, 1974); and Immanuel Wallerstein, *The Politics of the World-Economy: The States, the Movements, and the Civilizations* (Cambridge: Cambridge University Press, 1984).
52. For more comprehensive theoretical discussions, see and Thomas Clayton, "Explanations for the Use of Languages of Wider Communication in Education in Developing Countries," *International Journal of Educational Development* 18, no. 2 (1998): 145–57; and Thomas Clayton, "Beyond Mystification: Reconnecting World-System Theory for Comparative Education," *Comparative Education Review* 42 (November 1998).
53. Wallerstein, *The Politics of the World-Economy*, 15.
54. Francis T. MacNamara, *France in Black Africa* (Washington: Na-

tional Defense University, 1989), 92.

55. For a discussion of international publishing which illustrates the complexity of the contemporary world-system, see Daniel Johnson, "The Publishing World: Springtime for Bertelsmann," *The New Yorker*, 23 June–4 May 1998, 104–8.

56. Altbach and Kelly; Altbach and Rathgeber; and Altbach and Teferra.

57. Altbach, "Publishing in the Third World," 163.

58. Walter Bgoya, "The Challenge of Publishing in Tanzania," in *Publishing and Development in the Third World*, ed. Philip G. Altbach (London: Hans Zell Publishers, 1992), 169–90; and Zaline M. Roy-Campbell, "The Politics of Education in Tanzania," in *Tanzania and the IMF: The Dynamics of Liberalization*, eds. Horace Campbell and Howard Stein (Boulder, CO: Westview Press, 1992), 147–71.

59. Karen L. Biraimah, "Gender and Textbooks: An African Case Study," in *Textbooks in the Third World*, 118; for another relevant discussion, see A. Suresh Canagarajah, "Critical Ethnography of a Sri Lankan Classroom: Ambiguities in Student Opposition to Reproduction Through ESOL," *TESOL Quarterly* 27 (Winter 1993): 601–26.

60. Altbach, "Publishing in the Third World," 161.

61. Dennis Mbuyi, "Language and Texts in Africa," in *Textbooks in the Third World*, 167; for several examples, see Altbach and Kelly.

62. Biraimah, 139.

63. For general discussions of ideology in the world-system, see Robert F. Arnove, *Philanthropy and Cultural Imperialism: The Foundations at Home and Abroad* (Boston: G.K. Hall, 1980); Edward H. Berman, *The Influence of the Carnegie, Ford, and Rockefeller Foundations on American Foreign Policy: The Ideology of Philanthropy* (Albany: State University of New York Press, 1983); Mark B. Ginsburg, ed., *Understanding Educational Reform in Global Context: Economy, Ideology, and the State* (New York: Garland Publishing, 1991).

64. Robert Phillipson, *Linguistic Imperialism* (Oxford: Oxford University Press, 1992). Also see Hans R. Dua, *The Hegemony of English: The Future of Developing Languages in the Third World* (Mysore, India: Yashoda Publications, 1993); and Alastair Pennycook, *The Cultural Politics of English as an International Language* (London: Longman, 1994).

65. For example, Andrew Conrad, "The International Role of English: The State of the Discussion," in *Post-Imperial English: Status Change in Former British and American Colonies, 1940–1990*, eds. Joshua Fishman, Andrew Conrad, and Alma Rubal-Lopez (Berlin: Mouton de Gruyter, 1996).

66. Melvin Fox, *Language and Development: A Retrospective Survey of Ford Foundation Language Projects, 1952–1974* (New York: Ford Foundation, 1975). On the Ford Foundation and the Cold War project, see Arnove and Berman.

67. For example, Hutchison and Weinstein, "Language Planning in Francophone Africa."

Contributors

Philip G. Altbach directs the Bellagio Publishing Network's Research and Information Center. He is the Monan Professor of Higher Education and Director of the Center for International Higher Education at Boston College, Chestnut Hill, Massachusetts, USA.

Damtew Teferra is a doctoral candidate in higher education at Boston College, USA. He was the secretary of the African Association of Science Editors—Ethiopian Chapter. He has also served several scholarly associations in Ethiopia in different editorial capacities.

Urvashi Butalia is publisher at Kali for Women Publishers, New Delhi, India.

Thomas Clayton is an assistant professor of English at the University of Kentucky, Lexington, Kentucky, USA.

M.M. Mulokozi is a professor at the Institute for Kiswahili Studies—IKS, University of Dar es Salaam, Tanzania.

Dumisani K. Ntshangase is on the staff of Juta Publishers, Bedfordview, South Africa.

Victor U. Nwankwo is Managing Director of Fourth Dimension Publishers, Enugu, Nigeria. He is a founder of the African Publishers' Network (APNET).

Mamadou Aliou Sow is Director of Les Editions Ganndal, Conakry, Guinea.